THE
Hidden Power
OF
Sound

T0018252

THE
Hidden Power
OF
Sound

Love, Science & Mastery of Your Creative Spirit

Elizabeth Clare Prophet

SUMMIT UNIVERSITY 🕊 PRESS®

Gardiner, Montana

The Summit Lighthouse
63 Summit Way, Gardiner, MT 59030
Tel: 406-848-9500
www.SummitLighthouse.org
www.ElizabethClareProphet.com

Library of Congress Control Number: 2022934593
ISBN: 978-1-60988-396-6
ISBN: 978-1-60988-397-3 (eBook)

SUMMIT UNIVERSITY 🌿 PRESS®

Summit University Press, 🌿, *Pearls of Wisdom*, Keepers of the
Flame, the Threefold Flame logo and The Summit Lighthouse are
trademarks registered in the U.S. Patent and Trademark Office
and in other countries. All rights reserved.

Picture Credits:
Page 72: Guru Rinpoche (Padmasambhava) / creativecommons.
org/licenses/by/4.0/ Wellcome Library, London
Page 107: Tetragrammaton scripts / creativecommons.org/licenses/
by-sa/2.0/ Zappaz; Bryan Derksen

25 24 23 22   1 2 3 4

CONTENTS

DECREES AND MANTRAS

- 1 -

SOUND:
LIFE'S INTEGRATING PHENOMENON

For thousands of years the sacred texts of India have taught that sound holds the key to the mysteries of the universe, to the creation and sustaining of our world, and to the means of extricating ourselves from its bonds. In the Eastern tradition, the world of phenomenon is seen as a reflection of the infinite combinations of sound patterns, all derived from the soundless sound of the One who creates.

In order to explore the nature of sound, we will have to correlate the sciences of biology, atomic physics, chemistry, and mathematics, because sound is the integrating phenomenon. It is the common denominator through which and by which everything else operates. It will take a certain stretching of our minds to embrace the true nature of this creative sound.

Soundless Sound

Indian metaphysics explains that sound is the cause and not the effect of vibration and that there can be sound without vibration—even without the usual medium of conveyance such as air, water, or so-called solid matter. This is the concept of "potential sound"—the driving energy and force behind all manifestation. It is considered an infinite, endless continuum—indivisible, unfragmented, and potent—the most powerful source of all.

The power within the atom's core is but a minute pinpoint of this infinite energy, yet even this is able to destroy cities and even planets with its power. With the exception of the work of a handful of advanced scientists, such as Nikola Tesla and John Keely, the relatively coarse instruments of modern science have barely begun to probe this energy source.

This soundless sound is the subtlest element—finer than earth, air, fire, or water, beyond the speed of light, all pervasive, the source of cohesion, of electricity, of magnetism, of all that is.

The origin of sound, of the Word, of the divine name, reveals the entire story of creation. Indian metaphysics points to a primordial state from which creation emanates. By God's ever-creative impulse for self-transcendence, there was begun a causal stress that first created the primal sound known in Sanskrit as *para śabda*—*para* meaning "supreme" and *śabda* meaning "sound."

We will digress just a moment to understand what is meant by "stress" in this terminology. By definition, if two things are affecting one another, then the name of the total mutual action is stress. The respective actions of each are considered the partial aspects or components of the stress combination. This, of course, has nothing to do with emotional stress. On the contrary, we are considering the primary functioning of all sound and all form.

This concept actually forms the foundation of the philosophy of Taoism, founded in China by Lao Tzu around 590 B.C. It is the principle of yin-yang, the relationship of opposing or interacting forces. We can imagine a system of interactions involving two, three, four, or an infinite combination of elements or partial stress components. Ultimately, we reach the Eastern perspective of the physical universe as a vast conglomerate of interacting currents of energy, each supplying its particular factors of vibrational rate, direction, and angular momentum.

When the interacting stress between two such currents impinges upon our ears, we may perceive it as audible sound. When the energy system touches the retina of our eyes, it affects our mind and we call it light. The same is true for smell, taste, touch, and even thought patterns. For the mind has been described as a hard crystal of sound acting as a spherical reflector, receiving and radiating all of experience—conscious and subconscious.

Whether or not a particular śabda or stress results in a cognizable sensory reaction depends on two factors: the magnitude of its action in relation to the person affected by it, and the nature and condition of the person's perceptive organs—and ultimately, the refinement of the mind. Therefore, in order to have audible sound, the air must vibrate at a certain rate and the ear must receive the oscillations with a certain strength.

It is not too difficult to understand that though there may be a vibrational stress system, the outer ear may not perceive it as audible sound, because for this to happen, a certain amount of energy has to convey enough stress on the eardrum to make it vibrate. This is why the ordinary man does not hear a rock or the sun or the music of the spheres.

But man is able to become more aware of finer and finer vibrations. A being who can experience the causal stress, the Alpha and Omega primal interaction, can hear and know all things. The sphere of this potential sound has been the goal of yogic practitioners, adepts, and esoteric brotherhoods since time began.

The Initiatic Ladder

An example of one who sought the ultimate and sublime soundless sound through the initiatic steps, traversing matter and Spirit, was Robert Fludd—great Hermetic philosopher, Rosicrucian, and alchemist of the seventeenth century. Many of his writings and drawings reflected the beliefs of the esoteric guilds and mystery schools of the Great White Brotherhood.*

A depiction of Jacob's ladder drawn by Fludd shows the ladder of perfection and the steps to be taken to climb from the earthly realm to the highest heaven. It proceeds upward in geometrically measured steps— from the lowest rung of the senses to the world of imagination, then through reason to intellect (the ability of inner knowing), upward to intelligence (oneness with the object of direct knowing), and finally to the sacred Word itself, which leads into the heaven world. The meditation of alchemists and saints has always been upon that Word, upon its light, and ultimately, upon its inner sound.

For centuries, adepts East and West have practiced

---

*The Great White Brotherhood is a fraternity of ascended masters, archangels and other spiritual beings. The term "white" refers not to race but to the aura of white light that surrounds them. The Great White Brotherhood works with earnest seekers of every race, religion, and walk of life to assist humanity. The Brotherhood also includes certain unascended disciples of the ascended masters.

This drawing of Jacob's ladder, an ancient mystical symbol, depicts the levels of spiritual initiations required to advance from the earthly realm of the senses to the sacred Word, the doorway to heaven. The rungs of the ladder are (1) the senses, (2) imagination, (3) reason, (4) intellect, (5) intelligence, and (6) the Word.

the science of sound to become one with the Word. This timeless science does not confine its practitioners to physical or even nonphysical energy fields. Its techniques apply to all planes of being and are designed to transport the individual consciousness from the point of the Logos through the miasma of programmed sets of beliefs to a greater and greater proximity to the sphere of First Cause, supreme knowledge.

Once brought to this sphere of potential sound through the use of mantras and their careful *japa* (repetition), the mind internalizes the Source and becomes aware of the self as the Self of God. Some have called this state of God Self-awareness "cosmic consciousness." It is reached through the soundless sound of the Word.

The Tantric tradition, in its classical literature and practice, is designed for this purpose: the soul's approximation to the infinite Spirit. This is not the tantrism of perverted, erotic symbolism so misused today but the science of the yogic masters who have conquered time and space and left their footprints on the sands of time that we might follow.

Hindu Cosmogony

Esoteric tradition has always maintained that there is a symmetrical geometry to the evolution of cosmos. The great philosophers and observers have recognized the underlying order of creation.

This mathematical, evolutionary scheme has been depicted in the art and hieroglyphs of ancient manuscripts of diverse cultures. The ancient source of all Hindu cosmogony, called the Book of Dzyan, begins with a circle, then a point, then two straight lines. This symbolizes the unfolding sequence of the creative sound as it is stepped down to form all of cosmos.

The circle represents Brahman. It is the undivided, undifferentiated oneness of God before the formation of the worlds. The point is *para śabda,* the Word issuing as the first vibration pulsating in the cosmic womb. A point cannot enclose three-dimensional

Hindu symbols representing the unfolding sequence of creative sound from the undifferentiated oneness of God through denser octaves of vibration to the final manifestation of audible sound.

space. This point then is the germinal seed in the process of becoming.

The next emanation in this creative scheme is called *paśyanti* in the Hindu scriptures and is represented geometrically by straight lines. Paśyanti is a slightly denser octave of sound vibration. It is the plane where the relations and full meaning of all sound are revealed to the exalted consciousness. It is discriminative—hearing and cognition at its highest levels. At this stage, three dimensions have still not been enclosed diagrammatically.

The third step-down of primordial sound is called *madhyamā*. At this level, there are enough axes of direction that triangulation can occur. This represents the fundamental pattern of currents of sound diversifying as form. Comprehension of madhyamā sound offers intuitive insight. Hearing at this level means that we are perceiving meaning beyond the outer surface of the object or thought pattern.

Finally we come to *vaikharī* sound. This is the plane of audible sounds in nature as well as in articulated speech. It is the last stage in the densification of the causal sound. It varies according to how the medium of conveyance, such as air, is affected by the cause of the sound. The cause could be the human vocal cords or a tree falling to the ground.

Vaikharī operates at the level of so-called physical matter. The vaikharī sounds are the furthest diversification of the original sound. These are the words and letter sounds we use daily.

As summarized in the Yoga-kundalini Upanishad, "That VAK (power of speech) which sprouts in Para gives forth leaves in Paśyanti, buds forth in Madhyamā, and blossoms in Vaikharī."[1]

You can imagine the mind of God conveying the vastness of infinite vibrations—realizing that infinite vibrations produce infinite manifestations by the power of his Word. And his Word is the sound. A helpful analogy given by Swami Saraswati is that "as blood coagulates whenever it becomes manifest on the surface outside its inner container, so does sound coagulate into matter whenever it comes out of its earlier stages of para, paśyanti, and madhyamā."[2]

If one can attune to sound in its higher levels of madhyamā, paśyanti, and para, not only can he hear the musical tones of the planets described by Pythagoras but he can also hear the entire universe as it unravels with crystalline meaning. The whole cosmos is simply quivering in sound like the very quivering of many tiny leaves on a tree in spring or autumn. That quivering sound that makes us feel the movement of God is actually the universal comfort of life. This soundless sound is God's lullaby, and without it we would suddenly feel deserted and alone in space—without self-awareness and without contact with reality.

We can picture the first sound as a pure tone, a rhythmic pulsation. As more and more vibratory patterns are added to the first sound, the result can be likened to playing two or three or more notes on a piano. A chord, or combination of wave patterns, forms.

Our world, therefore, can be seen as a vast symphony of individual vibratory patterns, all interacting to create the warp and woof of substance. Each of the elements and substances of the universe is different because it is formed by a specific combination of vibrations. We can now begin to realize the vast power of the Word as it affects the very framework upon which all creation is hung.

2

PATTERNS OF CREATION

The course of man's history can be charted according to the nature of the relationship between the science and religion of society. As time proceeds, we are beginning to uncover the great truth that there is a unity of design underlying the basic principles of scientific and religious philosophy.

Let us gaze behind the scenes of creation to observe the geometry of God, usually hidden behind the veil of matter, and see visual evidence to support the once purely conceptual Indian viewpoint of sound as the creative source.

We're going to look at a series of images that are mainly the work of Hans Jenny, a Swiss doctor and scientist.[1] These images begin to give us an idea of how wave patterns of sound interact to form points of relationship—points that are the latticework of all substance.

In order to show the inner structure of sound, Jenny vibrated different substances at particular frequencies of sound and photographed the results. Figure 1 shows him with the apparatus he used to produce many of the following images of sound.

On the table in the foreground is a very thin, square steel plate about ten inches on a side. On the underside of the steel plate is an oscillator, a device that makes an audible sound. His left hand is touching a machine that allows him to vary the pitch from very low sounds to very high sounds.

In this photograph, he has placed sand on the plate. When the sound is turned on at the pitch he selects, the plate vibrates because of the sound, and patterns form in the medium used.

All of the different shapes of sound are simply the result of varying the pitch and loudness of the sound and the material put on the plate. There is no other contributing force in the creation of these patterns.

The sequence of images in figure 2 shows how a simple tone outpictures the shape of the inner pattern that composes it. In the upper left picture, sand is randomly diffused on a steel plate. As a tone of 7,560 cycles per second is introduced to the bottom of the plate, a transformation occurs.

FIGURE 1: In the Hindu tradition, sound has always been understood as the creative force from which emanates all matter. Although most scientists have discounted these religious beliefs, modern physicists have begun to realize that at the subatomic level all matter is in a state of constant motion—that matter is indeed energy at different rates of vibration and that by varying the rate of vibration, we can change the structure of matter. Looking at the work of Hans Jenny, Swiss doctor and scientist, gives us some insight into the mysterious process of creation. Jenny devised a specialized apparatus to vibrate sound through various media, capturing on film the harmonic and often beautiful patterns produced by sound.

The tone is audible throughout this process. We can actually see what we hear. Even more astounding is the notion that when we fully understand the workings of sound, we can begin to hear what we see.

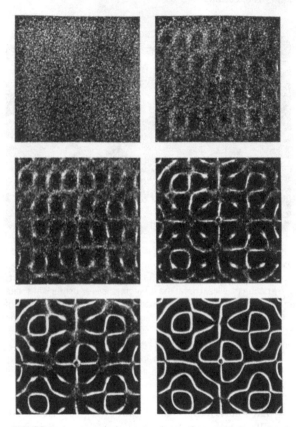

FIGURE 2: As a metal plate is made to vibrate with increasing intensity, sand that is initially distributed randomly takes on definite patterns.

FIGURE 3: As the pitch of a vibration increases, the basic pattern remains the same, but the number of elements increases. From top left to bottom right, the pitch changes from 1,690 to 2,500 to 4,820 to 7,800 beats per second.

In figure 3 we see what happens when the pitch, or rate of vibration, is increased from 1,690 to 2,500 to 4,820 to 7,800 cycles per second. The shape of the pattern stays the same, but the number of elements increases.

Figure 4 shows a pattern of sand particles on a circular plate vibrating at 8,200 cycles per second.

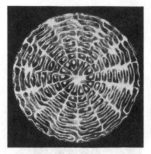

FIGURE 4: Sand on a circular plate vibrating at 8,200 cycles per second

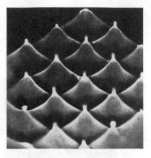

FIGURE 5: When sand is replaced by a liquid, different patterns emerge.

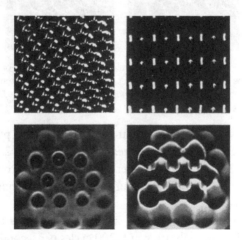

FIGURE 6: Many different regular patterns are formed when different sounds are used to vibrate liquid films.

Figure 5 shows what occurs when liquid is vibrated with sound—there is a weaving effect. Figure 6 shows some of the numerous different latticework patterns that result from various sounds. There are squares, many-sided polygons, all with a great orderliness. This type of effect is produced even at microscopic levels. The patterns are there as you increase the magnification hundreds of times. Imagine how sound produces its patterns in all of the interpenetrating dimensions.

When we place Hans Jenny's remarkable photographs side by side with those of cellular development, it is easy to see how sound could be the underlying force behind the patterns of creation.

On the left side of figure 7 are photographs of cellular life in different stages of cell division. The images on the right side show what happens when a round conglomeration of paste is vibrated with sound. The similarity is astounding.

The photographs in figure 8 show us some of the geometry and beauty of sound. Note the symmetry and how there is always a center, or nexus. The different shapes are due to varying the pitch and loudness of the sound. These forms are in a state of pulsation and movement. As the tone persists, there is a constant movement of the whole as it seeks to reach a point of perfect wholeness and symmetry.

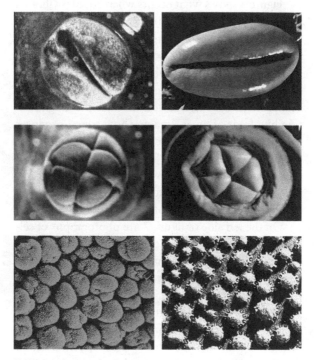

FIGURE 7: Stages of cell division are shown on the left, the effect of sound at various frequencies on the right.

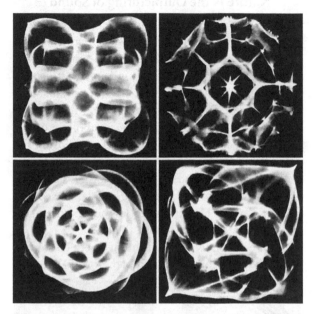

FIGURE 8: A stroboscope captures these intricate yet beautifully symmetrical interactions of various amplitudes of sound waves passing through a liquid. These figures are in a constant state of flow. Rotary waves often emerge and set the pattern turning.

Nature Is the Outpicturing of Sound

In order to deepen our understanding of some of the universal patterns forming the substructure of matter, let's look at a nineteenth-century carving of a very ancient Eastern concept, shown in figure 9. It depicts the *Bindu,* the point from which originates all sound in the cosmos. Those who meditated on this *yantra,* or geometric pattern, realized the symbology of the symmetrical, concentric rings as the eternal flow of the divine Word in creation.

Vibrate a liquid and the resulting form is shown on the right. As we look at them side by side, we see that the origin of the Hindu concept of the seed of sound can be illustrated using sound.

Figure 10 shows a beautiful five-petaled flower. Notice the pentagonal symmetry of the form. The image

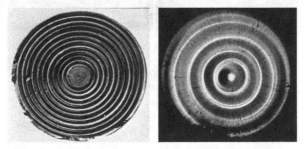

FIGURE 9: A Hindu carving depicting the emanating point of the Word of creation (left) echoes an excited liquid (right).

FIGURE 10: A beautiful flower pattern is reflected in this pentagon formed by a drop of water vibrating at yet another frequency.

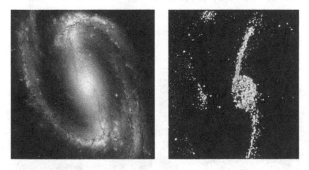

FIGURE 11: The spinning pattern of this starry galaxy is duplicated when sound waves are vibrated through sand on a steel plate. Dr. Jenny explains that "the rounded heaps of sand must be imagined in motion. The sand is flowing in the two longitudinal areas; it is flowing towards the round shape and joining it at opposite ends."

on the right shows this same five-petaled form created by sound. The inner geometry is evidently the same.

Figure 11 shows a photograph of a spiral galaxy 61 million light-years away and 110,000 light-years in width. The image on the right shows what happens when a frequency of 12,470 cycles per second is pulsated through a specific medium—sand on a steel plate. Macrocosm and microcosm, the sound of Elohim and the song of an audible tone.

Figure 12 shows an electron micrograph of a latticework of individual atoms in a crystal structure. We are actually looking at the patterns that create what the physical eye perceives as solid matter. On the right, we see a latticework of sound. It is not a very hard conceptual step to take to imagine that sound

FIGURE 12: An electron micrograph of individual atoms in a crystal structure (left) and a pattern produced by sound (right)

itself has caused the atoms to take up their pattern, that so-called hard matter is hung on the framework of sound—or even that hard matter *is* the framework of sound.

As we meditate upon the atoms and the sound, we have a sense of great internal harmony, we feel the tremendous comfort flame that is really behind everything that is outpictured, which we call science. The science of matter is really the precipitation of the comfort flame in our life.

In figure 13 we see the high, arching ceiling of a great Gothic cathedral. The builders of these masterpieces of architecture were often associated with esoteric Masonic guilds that had access to the knowledge of sacred geometry. Again, sound waves outpicturing

FIGURE 13: This magnificent ceiling of a Gothic cathedral on the left is mirrored in the sound-created pattern on the right.

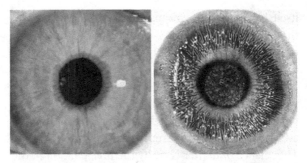

FIGURE 14: Photographs of a human eye and a pattern produced as a crescendo of sound vibrates through powder.

their inner form. Note the harmony, the similarity, between the ceiling and the sound.

Life is so amazingly harmonious and ordered that its very contemplation produces within us an inner sense of well-being and of being at home in a cosmos that is ordered, harmonious, and at peace with the interflow of light.

The image on the left in figure 14 is a photograph of an eye. The image on the right is a pattern created by sound.

Figure 15 is a photograph of a dynamic structure formed by the pulsation of sound through a kaolin paste. The vibration has caused the paste to become more liquid and to take on this shape. As the sound is turned off, the paste reverts to a semisolid mass.

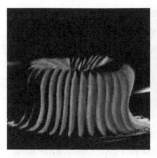 

FIGURE 15: A semisolid mass of kaolin paste forms itself into this dynamic structure as sound vibrates through it.

FIGURE 16: Under the influence of sound, milk easily defies the force of gravity.

This figure is in a state of movement. The radial patterns are actually the circulating flow of the doughlike matter traveling upward and inward.

In figure 16 we see how sound defies the force of gravity. By the vibratory action of the tone, this milk is climbing up into the air.

To me this illustrates that there is always an element of free will and creativity in matter, in electrons, in particles of substance. There is an element of consent—even in the most elemental life. The particles, instantaneously obedient to the sound, are obedient by conscious free will. Free will actually extends to all substance because the universal mind itself is free will. All that emanates therefrom contains that element.

Therefore, there is no mechanical world view. There is no reality to a mechanized universe. But because the love of all substance, energy, being, consciousness is so intense for the primordial Word and primordial sound, obedience is instantaneous and therefore has the appearance of mechanization.

The T'ai Chi (figure 17) is the ancient symbol of the interplay of opposite forces; the idea of the flow of yin and yang is embodied in this figure. This same flowing pattern emerged when sound was vibrated through powder. The powder in the pattern is being arranged by sound. This is a static photograph; the powder is actually in flowing motion. Meditating upon this through the heart, we have the sense of the

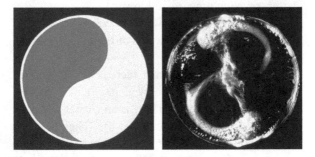

FIGURE 17: The T'ai Chi symbolizes the interplay of cosmic forces, the yin-yang polarity underlying all manifestation. This same flowing pattern emerged when sound was vibrated through powder.

movement of Alpha and Omega that produces the causal stress.

The Inner Sound of the Word

The Eastern sages tell us that all matter is actually the interplay of waves of sound. We have seen in these images how sound creates form and geometrical patterns.

It is not such a big step, then, to reach the realization that all form in nature is the outpicturing of causative sound. If God as the Creator can form and change the vast array of the plane of Matter, we as co-creators can use the science of sound to form and change the patterns of the world and our inner beings.

The inner sound of the Word is the sound that I have heard—not only in this life, but in previous lives. The overwhelming meditation of my soul has been upon this inner sound, which is a vibration and not a vibration, a presence and yet, somehow, a presence that is not defined in the ordinary sense of the word.

When the chakras are refined and the bodily senses are purified, we become instruments like tuning forks— perpetually vibrating, distributing, emanating this inner sound. And when we have the inner sound, we are ever listening in listening grace, with the Blessed Mother, to the word of life that flows forth in, as, and through this inner sound.

According to Indian metaphysics, the rarified plane of cosmos is not only the source of sound but its destination as well. All proceeds from its potency. And all that is apparent, or manifest, ultimately returns to it. To become one with this force, to know its workings, is to gain access to all knowledge.

When the sound crystal of the mind is dissolved and resolved into unity with this creative matrix of manifestation, we then have mastery of this mortal realm because all power in heaven and earth has become accessible.

3

THE SACRED AUM

M editating on the sphere of the soundless sound, we intuit that light is actually a particular spectrum of the vibrations of sound. Depending on the frequency and angular relationships of the wave patterns, this sound becomes either gas, liquid, or solid. Beyond these three dimensions of coagulated sound are many other planes—as numerous as God is infinite in his creative potential, and as far as the outbreath of the *manvantara* has proceeded.

Every object or being has its own seminal sound, or *bija* mantra, which contains the blueprint of the energy patterns that compose it. Over thousands of years, ancient tradition has brought forth the bija sounds of many of the most exalted beings, as well as the elements of earth, air, water, and fire. By performing *japa,* or repetition, with a bija mantra, we create a harmonic resonance with the being or element whose seminal sound is that bija mantra.

In a linguistic sense, bijas have no meaning in and
of themselves. But mantra yogis fully realize that the
shakti, or potent force of the divine being, is transmit-
ted to the one who is chanting the mantra.

The bija sound for the earth element is LAM (lăm).
The bija sound for water is VAM. The bija sound for
air is YAM. Fire is the sound RAM. Ether, or *akasa,*
has the bija sound HAM. As we give these bija mantras, we can attune to the inner pattern of each plane
of God's being.

Each one of these five sounds ends in the letter *M,*
which is the sound of Mother, or MA. It is the sound
of the HUM (hōōm) of the Mother flame, and it is the
sound that crystallizes what is coming forth from the
causal stress into physical matter. Mother is the author
of the *Mater* universe.

The first letter of each bija denotes its frequency.
The central vowel of each of these bijas is *A*—the
action of Alpha, or the Father principle. The Father
creates, the Mother seals the creation. The three letters
of each bija form the Trinity—the Trinity that is always
necessary to have a seed.

The sound for earth is LAM—the *AM* denoting the
Be-ness of the Father-Mother God in manifestation.
AM is preceded by the letter *L*—the letter of God,
Elohim. One can imagine Elohim intoning this sound

for the formation of earth itself.

This *M* is sounded high up in the nasal cavity. It is the culmination of the bija mantra, which begins in the solar plexus area and is unfolded upwards until it is sent off into the ethers sealed in the *M* sound.

The sacred fire breath that we breathe when we intone the Word actually is a funnel within the entire cavity of our being. The consonant or first letter cannot be pronounced without the vowel sound. The vibration produced by *M* at the end of bijas is meant to leave the body in such a way that there is no sharp cut off as the sound flows into space.

Using the Word

Dipping into the vast ocean of Indian metaphysics, into which we have barely dipped our toes, we can draw certain conclusions that will form the foundation for our understanding of just how we may use the Word to effect change in our own lives and in the world as a whole.

First: All objects—whether thoughts, ideas, or the grossest matter—are concentrated and coagulated patterns of sound waves interacting to form a lattice framework of nuclear energy centers.

Second: Every object is the result of a specific pattern and density of sound that may be called the seminal, or bija, sound. The seminal sound is the seed. If this seminal sound is likened to the seed of a tree, then the manifested object is analogous to the tree that is the outpicturing of the seed's potential.

Third: There is an octave of sound within every object that originates in the plane of causal stress. The octave's lower end is in the plane of matter.

Fourth: By knowing the seminal sound of an object or manifestation, we can not only fully experience it, but we can also remold or destroy it because we can then actually change its wave patterns.

Fifth: By the ultimate knowledge of sound, man can not only create but he can also sustain and destroy.

This is why the masters and gurus of the East require long periods of testing and proving of their chelas before each level of greater power can be bestowed by the giving of the inner secrets of the Word. Nevertheless, the use of sound is available unto anyone who makes the effort—and upon the magnitude of effort rests the degree of control, power, and spiritual attunement that comes into our lives.

The Bija of God

As the bija of God himself, the AUM represents the unified envelope of sound that is the combination of all the disjointed individual sounds careening through the

This yantra has been used for many centuries in the East to represent
the AUM, the mantra of mantras.

cosmos. Put another way, all sounds—and therefore
all experience and being—are derived from the AUM.

AUM is the seed syllable of Brahman. AUM is the
sound of the beating of God's heart in perfect equilib-
rium. AUM is the first sound and the last. All issued
from it, all returns to it. This is why yogis have forever
recognized it as the mantra of mantras.

Perfect unity with AUM means perfect union with God. And this is the goal of all yoga—which means union. Perfect unity with the AUM means perfect love, perfect harmony, perfect truth, perfect peace. These are qualities we, of our free will, summon and bring to the AUM.

Each one of us pronouncing the AUM is creating something a little bit different, a different sound pattern, because what we focus in the sound represents the sum total of our being—all that we have ever been back to the first incarnation upon earth and even back to our origin in the Word.

When we breathe out the sacred fire breath in the AUM, our identity can be defined by any Elohim who hears that sound. As we know our mother's voice, so God knows the vibration of his children.

Your sounding of the AUM is the call to God that says, "I am coming Home." It lets God know that everything that you are, you are sending back to him with the deepest and most intense love.

The more love you feel, the more gratitude and joy when you sound the AUM, the more you are going to reach the far-off worlds, the farthest stars, and even the Great Central Sun of the cosmos. The simple illustration that a single candle can be seen almost infinitely reminds us that the single sound we make can also be heard infinitely.

When we flow with the Word and we feel the presence of the Holy Spirit and we realize that millions of angels and ascended masters and saints on high and cosmic beings worlds beyond worlds have all attained to where they are (to their state of "Be-ness") by the science of the spoken Word and that we have in our hands this very gift of the teaching of the Great White Brotherhood, why, all we have to do is go to work, roll up our sleeves, and enter in to this very joyous work of the ages—every sound creating all that is like God, every sound uncreating all that is unlike him.

You can send a message to God of your deepest love and gratitude by simply sending to him the AUM of your soul. Now there is no longer any doubt that wherever God is, whoever God is, wherever the focal point of consciousness is, that He is. Wherever I AM THAT I AM, your AUM is heard, your AUM has made contact.

It is the ancient story of the sacred sound. It is His story of the sound of the Word. That knowledge becomes power—the power of love within us. How can any turn aside from it? How can any deny it? How can any do anything but simply flow with it and keep on flowing through the great cosmic ocean of God's being?

4

RESONATING WITH THE WORD

In the Indian view of the cosmos, the whole universe is an ocean of sound and light of varying degrees of density or luminosity. It is understood that sound precedes even light.

If we vibrate a glass rod with ultrasonic vibrations (those having a frequency beyond the audibility of the human ear), the glass gives off heat and light. Before our eyes we see sound producing fire and light—an example of what could be called the soundless sound precipitating as fire and light.

As we experiment with the science of the spoken Word, we experience—with the "glass rod" of the body itself—the causal relationship of sound to the heat of spiritual fire and the light and en*light*enment of spiritual light for the transmutation of all obstacles to our accelerating consciousness.

When we refine our chakras and the bodily senses, we can become tuning forks—perpetually vibrating, distributing, emanating the sacred Word. We, in the hand of God, become the glass rod that he vibrates with his soundless sound. We experience the effect as the heat of transmutation, as the light permeating atoms of the brain, the chakras, the soul. Thus, the acceleration of consciousness comes from God emitting the soundless sound and holding us in a vast cosmos as rods, cones, cells, atoms of his being.

Tuning In to God

When I talk to young people and I see people so distressed and so burdened by life, I always want to impart the joy that "God is here and now the very answer to all of your needs and all of your cares." It just takes tuning in. For God has created us as tuning forks to resonate with his Word. And this magnificent body that we wear in all of its miraculous functioning, particle by particle, is the precipitation by sound of every organ, every cell, everything that we need to be a functioning microcosm within the Macrocosm.

If you just study the body itself and look at what it contains and realize that all of its interconnecting parts, all of its systems working together in harmony, are the result of God sounding a tone—many tones, the great symphony of life itself—and you look at yourself and you say, "Why, I am a crystallized symphony of life!"

then life becomes exciting moment by moment and
you can't wait to experiment with the Word.

When we give prayers and mantras written and
spoken by the avatars and saints of all ages whom we
call the ascended masters, their very essence is injected
into the sound of the Word. We are going straight
through *maya* (the planes of illusion) to beings who are
one with the Source, who have returned to the Source
(the very nucleus of the atom, the Atman of the Higher
Self) by the sacred sound.

And therefore we experience an uninterrupted
flow whereby that specific vibration of the Word,
personalized in the mantra of the saint, flows from
heaven to earth (from the positive to the negative pole
of being) because we have determined that this temple
shall be the temple of the living God—a channel for
the ever-flowing River of Life.

When you give a mantra of Jesus Christ, Gautama
Buddha, Mother Mary or Saint Francis, Maitreya or
Padma Sambhava, or any accelerated being whose soul
has become a part of the eternal Spirit, the I AM THAT
I AM, that Holy One of God, by the conquering of the
Word, is where you are, giving the mantra through
you. By the sound and the rhythm, you are one. There
is no separation. Wherever God is, your AUM is heard,
your AUM has made contact.

So sound is the great command. And when you send forth the sound of the perfect AUM of the Word, and when you yourself are in perfect love for all life, all life must respond to you in obedience to the command of the AUM.

Science Confirms Faith

We can see then how an understanding of the science of sound and its mathematics confirms our faith that prayer does indeed work, that dynamic decrees are the most intense release of the fire of our meditation.

The images in chapter 2 give us the inner visualization that we cannot utter the sacred name of God without a corresponding manifestation in every single atom and cell of our being. Every cell becomes a temple to the living God where a flame burns and rises and pulsates to the rhythm of our sounding of the AUM. When we say AUM, a billion fiery candles are burning upon the altar of this body temple, and every cell becomes a macrocosm where angels may enter, and cosmic beings may consort with us.

Suddenly we realize that we are a universe and a galaxy all inside, and in the very center of our heart is the Central Sun. And that which is spoken, derived from the heart, passes through the heart and manifests instantaneous creation, preservation, and the dissolution of those worlds within us that were not framed by the Word of God, but by the lesser misuse of the Word.

Therefore, we can see how galaxies and solar systems within this body can be created and collapsed at will. We can realize that God has given to us a most magnificent temple, that if we keep it pure and unde-filed, and take in only pure substances and meditate upon God, we can begin the spiral of prolonging life, strengthening life, having healthier bodies, having temples that can give birth to more noble archetypes of individuals and evolutions destined to embody upon earth in the coming golden ages. We see that with the science of sound, God has made us unlimited co-creators with him.

Opportunity for a Vast Creation

The sounding of the name of God in its many forms —the Hebrew El Shaddai, the Sanskrit AUM, the English I AM THAT I AM—gives us the opportunity for a vast creation. We find that the sounding of that name assures us that we are an integral part of God and eternity here and now. The sounding of the names of God and the seed syllables of the attributes of his consciousness delivers us from *samsara,* which is the valley of personal and planetary karma in the dark cycle of the Kali Yuga.

We don't have to sit and wait for something to happen, for a deliverer, for the Word to incarnate. We don't have to wait until we get past this struggle or that problem or this burden to realize God. Rather, we displace all of that which appears as struggle, with the sounding of the Word where we are. And as soon as we sound the Word, we are no longer in an incomplete state where all is suffering through impure desire. The sounding of the Word means the Word is where I AM.

Why, God has been vibrating the spheres with that Word for eternity! And when you the co-creator return the Word to the Creator, when you the creation have become one with the Creator, then time and space collapse; for they are mere coordinates for those who have engendered the mode of a self-styled, separate identity from the unity of life.

For you—if you will it so—the prison house of time and space can cease to exist here and now. And from this point of light for the rest of this incarnation of the Word, you can experience the sheer joy of eternity.

And if you do not, it is merely because you have not exercised the potency of the Word that you are.

5

IN THE BEGINNING . . .

Receiving the Word of the LORD and only taking in the intellectual level—and for thousands of years people have been discerning God intellectually—is not enough; it is not soul-satisfying. So if our souls are to be nourished, we need to meditate upon the Word and take in the Word in all of the seven planes of being, in the seven chakras.

It is not the words, words, words that you can repeat that will give you the marks when you stand before the Lords of Karma at the conclusion of this life—it is the Word that you have become. And so this is the great joy and the gift that the ascended masters have given to their chelas in this century—the gift of the incarnate Word.

We can't possess the Word. We can only become the Word. One cannot possess it unless one has become it. So if you visualize yourself not as a dense flesh-and-blood body but actually as a grid or forcefield like a latticework, then as the sacred fire of the Word and the sacred name pass through you, there is a cleansing action. And when the cleansing is fulfilled then there is the building from the foundation to the top of a new identity—your new identity in the Word.

Each one who receives the Word receives it for whatever purpose is required, and all purposes of the alchemy of God cannot be fulfilled at once because we are in different states of evolution. So the teaching that is given can be heard again and again and again because the coils and spirals of the Word continue to work their work in us.

In the end, what you have become is what you will have the ability to transfer to others. And that is the purpose of our path. It is not a selfish path. The only reason for becoming the Word is that we might impart that Word to those who need the nourishment of life.

The Nature of God

In the beginning was Brahman, with whom was the Word. And the Word is Brahman.[1]

Thousands of years after this verse was recorded in one of the world's oldest religious texts, the Vedas of ancient India, John the Beloved began the fourth gospel with these words:

In the beginning was the Word, and the Word was with God, and the Word was God.[2]

As we meditate upon this Word and realize that it is inseparable from God as Brahman, we find that the Word is given that we might follow it back to the center, to the point of light that is the Being of God. Therefore, the intoning of the Word.

From the earliest periods of history, and in every corner of the globe, man has pondered the vast mysteries and the glories of the evolution of the universe. He has continued to reach into the depths of his being to understand the nature of his God, to embrace life's meaning, to become liberated from the bonds that prevent the unfettered flight of his soul.

Positioning ourselves in the Word, the pinions of the bird of the soul are poised to take flight. The soul, then, is ready to fly, ready to merge with the Word.

As we are ready, as this is our desiring, we kneel before the LORD and we ask, "How may I return to the center of the Word that is God and that was with God, Brahman, in the beginning?"

Brahman and the Word

Brahman is the Hindu equivalent of God. The meaning of *Brahman* is "the undivided, omnipresent One." It is God before the creation, before the emanation, before the manifestation of Brahma, Vishnu, and Shiva, before Father, Son, and Holy Spirit. It is the Absolute without attributes—simply God without description, without form, without even formlessness. It is this God, Brahman, with whom we find the Word. The Word is the sound-light emanation of Brahman, the creative sound that instantaneously becomes the creative light-manifestation of God.

The Word, the Logos, has always been the pivot point of man's highest understanding. It is through the Word that we arrive at Brahman. And the Word incarnate declares, "No man cometh to the Father but by me. I AM the open door which no man can shut." [3]

The Word that is in the beginning with God can be transferred to form, to formlessness. And therefore, Brahman becomes accessible to us only by the Word.

"In the beginning was the Word," and the self-creative Word of God is recorded as

Let there be light: and there was light.[4] [chanted]

As I speak that Word, the silence that follows is filled with the sound of this self-creative Word of God.

You can meditate upon the soundless sound that follows my speaking of this self-creative Word. The point of your meditation is your heart, which you visualize in the center of the chest cavity. The focal point of the light of the heart is, however, to the left, corresponding with the physical heart.

> *Let there be light: and there was light.* [pause]

The duration of the sound is until the moment of my speaking again. It is a roaring sound, an inner sound. It is not vibrating on the physical, and therefore it is called the soundless sound. It is heard with the inner ear.

Let us repeat it together and then observe the inner sound.

> *Let there be light: and there was light.* [pause]
>
> *Let there be light: and there was light.* [pause]
>
> *Let there be light: and there was light.* [pause]

The Vessel of the Word

The soul in you that desires to unite with the Word is wearing veils as the four lower bodies—the memory, the mind, the feelings, the physical body—which are comprised in themselves of many, many layers, like our skin. Skeins and skeins of energy intertwining compose the forcefield where your soul is positioned. All of these comprise the vessel, and the vessel is an instrument.

When the soul within the vessel pronounces the Word, or the mantra of the Word, the element of the Word that can manifest is conditioned by these veils. Therefore in this age the ascended masters have come to us with the means to accelerate and purify the veils, the coats of skins,[5] the vessel, so that when we sound the tone and the light goes forth, there is a greater and greater manifestation instantaneously crystallizing the Word.

The degrees of consciousness of hearing the Word depend upon the vessel, which is the vehicle whereby we can interpret and experience and experiment with the Word. Therefore it is an ongoing process.

Wherever you begin is the beginning, and it is a spiral that is created. And day by day by day, through the repetition of the self-creative Word, the self in you is being re-created, layer upon layer upon layer, until, as it is ordained, you are walking the earth in what would still be called a physical body, but you may walk the earth in your light body, the etheric body and even the garment known as the deathless solar body, which is the vehicle that prepares you for the ascension, which is the ultimate union with God.

I want you to remember the self-creative Word. It is also the re-creative Word. And it is this fiat, "In the beginning," that we use to establish that point of contact with the reality of the Word. Let us do it again.

> *Let there be light: and there was light.* [pause]
>
> *Let there be light: and there was light.* [pause]
>
> *Let there be light: and there was light.* [pause]

THE WORD IN THE VEDAS

In the creation myths of Hinduism and Brahmanism, which had such a pervasive influence on other religious cosmologies, we find the power of the Word referred to in Sanskrit as *Vak,* the primal influence of all creation.

The Vedas state that the union of the will and the Word was the potency of creation. We read:

> Prajapati [the Lord of Progeny] alone was this universe. He had Vak too as His own, as a Second to Him. He thought, "let me now put forth this Vak. She will traverse and pervade all this."[1]

In the Mahabharata, which contains the epic Bhagavad-Gita, Vak, the Word, is called the "Mother of the Vedas."[2] The word *Vedas* refers here not to only those monumental religious texts of ancient India but also to all knowledge in general.

The Upanishads are the sacred commentaries on the Vedas, which form the foundation of Vedanta philosophy, still prevalent in India and throughout the world. In one of these Upanishads it is said:

> By Vak, O monarch, the Brahman is known.
> Vak is the Supreme Brahman.[3]

Perhaps the greatest accomplishment in all of the vast discourses of the world's religious philosophies is the Hindu integration of the most abstract cosmological speculations with the most practical teachings, designed for each aspirant to climb to the highest summit of being. The Word not only plays the key role in the creative and evolutionary process, but it is also central to the most ancient and detailed techniques for self-mastery and liberation handed down for aeons from Guru to chela.

Hinduism is probably the only living example of a truly practical metaphysics because the actual techniques used in everyday practice by its adherents are integral with a so-called abstractions of its cosmologies.

Mantra Yoga

Mantra yoga is that body of knowledge in which the science of sound and the spoken Word are used to gain union with God, as he manifests as divine beings or as exalted spiritual attributes of himself.

Religious founders throughout the ages, saints, yogis, sages, and avatars, have repeatedly taught that by the use of the Word, or the divine name, one can most quickly reach the goal of life and become a co-creator. It is written in the Kali Santarana Upanishad:

> At the end of the Dvapara Yuga, Narada [disciple of Sanat Kumara] approached Brahma, the Creator, and said, "O Lord, how shall I be able to cross Kali, wandering in this world." Brahma replied, "Hearken that which the [sacred teachings] keep as secret and hidden, by which one may cross the Samsara in Kali Yuga. One can shake off the evil effects of Kali through the mere uttering of the Name of Lord Narayanya."[4]

Narayana is another name for Lord Vishnu—Christ. The mantra to Narayana has been given for thousands of years in the East: *Om Namo Narayanya,* meaning, "Praise be the name of Lord Narayana." Let us give it together.

Om Namo Narayanya

Om Namo Narayanya

Om Namo Narayanya

The practice of uttering the name of a divine being developed into the highly advanced science of *japa* yoga.

This yoga is the repetition of mantras that are combinations of words or names that form the vehicle for the aspirant to return to his Source in God or Brahman, the mighty I AM Presence, the Sun behind the sun, behind the manifest creation of Father, Son, and Holy Spirit.

Many of the sacred texts of India are replete with stories illustrating the power of the Word and the role it has played in history. For example, the goddess Kali destroyed innumerable demons with a certain kind of roaring sound.

A king named Venue, who was very powerful, began to rule immorally and was causing much consternation to the rishis. He was unconquerable on the

This eighteenth century manuscript painting depicts eight goddesses in battle against the demon Raktabija and his followers. Kali is seen consuming the demons by the power of her tongue.

battlefield. But the rishis knew and used the science of sound and certain patterns of mantras and proceeded to conquer the king and take over the kingdom from the evil one.

The great importance attached to the Word can be seen in an excerpt from the Chandogya Upanishad.

> The essence of all beings is earth. The essence of earth is water. The essence of water is plants. The essence of plants is man. The essence of man is speech. The essence of speech is the Rig-veda. The essence of the Rig-veda is the Sâma-veda. The essence of the Sâma-veda is the udgitha (which is Om).
>
> That udgitha (Om) is the best of all essences, the highest place, the eighth.[5]

In a later chapter of the Chandogya Upanishad, we read the account of a dialogue between the sage Narada and Sanat Kumara, who is regarded as the first Guru, the originator of the yogic discipline. Sanat Kumara says:

> "He who meditates on a name as Brahman can of his own free will reach as far as the name reaches —he who meditates on a name as Brahman."
>
> Narada said, "Venerable sir, is there anything greater than a name?"

Sanat Kumara replied:

"He who meditates on speech as Brahman can
of his own free will reach as far as speech reaches—
he who meditates on speech as Brahman."[6]

Sanat Kumara holds a very high position in classical Hindu theology. He appears as the Guru of gurus
in several ancient texts. Upon the framework of the
dialogues with his disciples has grown the knowledge
of yoga psychology and the purpose for austerities.
In this excerpt of the instruction to Narada, Sanat
Kumara equates name and speech with Brahman, the
undivided being of God.

7

THE WORD, EAST AND WEST

The secrets of the power of sound and of mantra repetition have been known in every culture, every religion, every mystery school throughout the ages. The rishis of the remote Himalayas, the magi of Persia, the priesthood of Egypt, the adepts of Babylonia, Hebrew rabbis, Christian clergy, all have recognized that the key that unlocks the doors to their respective concepts of heaven is the Word—spoken, sung, chanted, and offered in prayer.

There have been numerous forms in which man has used the Word to draw closer to God. The use of Gregorian chants was begun under Pope Gregory in the sixth century. This blending of sonorous melody and words of praise has continued for fourteen hundred years to the present.

Pythagoras, the great master of mathematics, astronomy, and philosophy, taught the essential curative powers of sound and the Word. He taught that

Pythagoras, detail from *The School of Athens*, by Raphael

all of creation was based on the harmony of numbers.

Pythagoras taught that the distance between the planets of our solar system was in proportion to the notes of the musical scale. He described a symphony of sound that emanated from the tones of the planetary movements and called it the music of the spheres.

Pythagoras would read mantric verses from Homer's *Odyssey* and other great epics to effect cures for the sick. By the power of his love carried upon the rhythmic and meaningful words of Homer, healing energy would flow forth.

Jesus would heal by the power and authority of his word.

> There came a leper to him, beseeching him,
> and kneeling down to him, and saying unto him,
> If thou wilt, thou canst make me clean.
> And Jesus, moved with compassion, put forth
> his hand, and touched him, and saith unto him,
> I will; be thou clean.[1]

Paul testifies of Jesus Christ "upholding all things by the word of his power."[2] It is written that Jesus "rebuked the wind, and said unto the sea, Peace, be still. And the wind ceased, and there was a great calm."[3]

In past centuries, common people in India would gather during droughts and famine and chant mantras together as a group—and the rain would come, and the grain would grow. The American Indians, invoking the Great Spirit, are known to have accomplished the control of the elements. High priests of the Mayan culture contacted their divine hierarchy by the use of the Word.

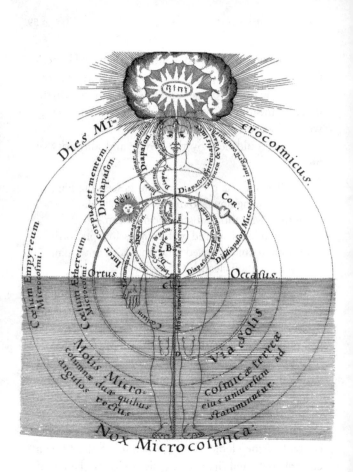

This diagram by Robert Fludd draws an analogy between the body of man and the spheres of the cosmos surrounding the planet.

Microcosm and Macrocosm

This diagram by Robert Fludd depicts the Pythagorean idea that there is a geometrical design of man as a microcosm and man as a macrocosm. The distances between the major anatomical features of the body and the distances between the planetary spheres are proportional. These proportions are also mathematically identical to the vibratory ratios that make the different musical notes.

Pythagoras made the brief statement, "All is number." Since number is a rate of vibration in the phenomenal world, he understood and taught the essence of the Indian science of sound, which we explored in earlier chapters.

It's interesting to note that the circle that passes through the heart area has on one side the Latin word *Sol,* meaning "sun," and on the other side *Cor,* meaning "heart." This shows the basic understanding that the I AM is the light of the heart, that the sun is the center of being—the Sun behind the sun as the I AM Presence.

The cloud of glory above the head of the man shows the crown chakra opening unto the mighty I AM Presence. It is the Shekhinah glory, and the Hebrew letters are the tetragrammaton, YOD HE VAU HE, the initials standing for I AM THAT I AM.

The Search for the Harmony of Life

We find that the harmony of life—inner and outer —has been sought by alchemists, mathematicians, scientists, and those who have been on the path of the inner cross, the inner fire; those who have found the secret chamber of the heart, the inner cathedral, and the inner communion; those who have understood that there is an inner light to be followed to its Source.

There are manuscripts in underground crypts of Himalayan monasteries that were preserved from before the Atlantean deluge. Madame Blavatsky brought these to the attention of the world through *The Secret Doctrine,* and James Churchward's series of books on Mu did the same.

We learn that Atlantean temples were used as great halls for the resonance of the spoken Word to go forth and perform its sacred functions. It is said that the sacred language, the language of Sensar, was used, and that Sanskrit is a derivative of Sensar.

Cycles of Planetary Evolution

There is a very ancient teaching in the East that explains the cyclic nature of man's spiritual and cultural evolution on the planet. It is understood that there are four related time cycles (*yugas* in Sanskrit) and that all of man's history reaching back millions

Atlantis, by Auriel Bessemer

of years can be traced along the crests and troughs of these evolutionary waves. The power of the Word has been known and used since the beginning of these historical lifewaves, but in each cycle a particular method of spiritualization was predominant.

The sacred scriptures say that in what is called the Satya Yuga, the techniques of meditation were prescribed by the gods as the principal form of spiritual discipline.

In the following Tretā Yuga, sacrifices as spiritual austerities were used due to the particular psychological makeup of mankind in that period. During the Dvāpara Yuga, the worship of the deity was the most efficacious path.

We are currently in what is called the Kali Yuga. According to the Indian scriptures, mankind today are less disciplined mentally and more prone to distractions of the mind than previous lifewaves.

Within the Kali Yuga is the Dark Cycle of the return of mankind's karma. When there is an acceleration of the return of karma as there was fourteen thousand years ago, before the sinking of Atlantis, there is a scattering of energies, absence of discipline, and the distractions that come from constant energies impinging upon the body, the chakras, the mind, and the heart.

So it is that in this yuga, mantra yoga—the use of the Word of God—has been recognized as the key technique for salvation. Bringing forward all of the forms of these four yugas, we find that meditation, sacrifices, and worship of the deity are all culminating and being released as the inner attainment of the soul through the science of the spoken Word.

The sages of old foresaw this, the cycle of the Word's supremacy. The adepts through the millennia knew and demonstrated the power of the spoken Word in its various forms. Now millions of people are waking up to this most exalted and spiritual of all the sciences—the science of the Word.

The Orthodox Stream and Tantra

There are basically two broad currents in the religious histories of India, Tibet, and the Far East. One is the orthodox, doctrinal, and literary tradition of Hinduism, Buddhism, and Jainism.

The other stream is known as Tantra. Tantrism consists of a vast religious literature that uses the basic metaphysical tenets of Hinduism and Buddhism, but whose origin is independent of any one system. It consists mainly of practices and techniques (as opposed to philosophical speculation) that had been used by yogis, ascetics, and spiritual aspirants in the East from the earliest times. The subject matter of the tantras consists of yoga, rituals, medicinal practices, magic, and most important of all, mantra yoga.

There are basically only two elements common to all Indian philosophy. First is the axiom of the metempsychosis of the soul (reincarnation) and the possibility of one's emancipation from the Wheel of Rebirth. Second is the notion of an Absolute underlying the diverse phenomenal universe, the concept of unity in diversity.

Of all the practices and contemplative exercises (called *sadhana*) that are used to gain liberation from the Wheel of Rebirth, it is the use of mantras and sound that is considered the most important.

Sri Shankaracharya, the greatest commentator on the Upanishads, lived in India in the eighth century. He declared that the essence of the Upanishadic dicta as, "This Atma is Brahma," "I AM Brahma," "Thou art that," and "The conscious self is Brahma."[4] He explained that to fully embrace this process of identifying with the Creator, or Brahma, was to ensure liberation.

There is a sacred mantra in Hinduism that means "I AM Brahma."

> *Aham Brahma Asmi*
> *Aham Brahma Asmi*
> *Aham Brahma Asmi*

The equivalent in English would be:

> *I AM THAT I AM*
> *I AM THAT I AM*
> *I AM THAT I AM*

8

MANTRA IN BUDDHISM

Though there are major disparities between Hindu-ism and Buddhism, both place a great emphasis on speaking the divine name and using the power of the Word. The appearance of Gautama Buddha in the sixth century B.C. came thousands of years after the early Vedas of Hinduism.

At the time of Buddha'a appearing, the teach-ings and practices of the Hindu faith were already entrenched and developed in India. As the case has been in the history of many major religions, a certain degree of stagnation and rigidity had set in. And to some extent, the Buddhist teachings were a reaction to the decadence and hypocrisy of a mundane Hindu priesthood. Instead of relying on the power from within, many Hindus began to expect a supernatural agent to do the work for them.

Gautama Buddha

Buddha's teachings emphasize the self-determination and self-responsibility of man and the need to strive for one's liberation. After a philosophical restructuring process to bestow the necessary self-discipline, Buddhist teachings began to pick up and further evolve the mantric techniques of Tantric Hinduism. Yoga was always a key part of Buddhism, and a continuous exchange took place between the two religious schools of thought.

Even though the AUM mantra had temporarily been disregarded by the Buddha, it is clear from historical records that the use of mantras was nevertheless taught by him as a means for awakening faith, for the liberation from hindrances, and for the reaching of the Supreme Goal.

In Majjhima Nikāya 86, a Buddhist text, Gautama has one of his disciples, a converted robber, cure a woman who was suffering from a difficult and painful labor by the power of a mantric utterance of truth. Throughout the career of the Buddha, he showed his disciples how a properly expressed thought pattern couched in a rhythmical, melodious, and forceful delivery could have powerful effects.

Let us give a mantra of Gautama Buddha.

AUM
Tatyata Om Muni Maha Muni Shakyamuniye Svaha
Tatyata Om Muni Maha Muni Shakyamuniye Svaha
Tatyata Om Muni Maha Muni Shakyamuniye Svaha
AUM

It was shown that the efficacy of such mantric formulas depends on the harmonious cooperation of form, feeling, and idea. If these are in balance, then the full power of the Word can manifest—form as the combination of sound and rhythm; feeling as devotion, faith, and love; idea as the holding of the proper attitude and mental associations concerning the goal.

It was fully understood in the Mantrayāna, or mantric schools of Buddhism, that a mechanical repetition of mantras would not bring the highest results, but that purity of heart and motive were necessary adjuncts to the practice.

The Jewel in the Lotus

One of the most sacred mantras that has come down to us in the Buddhist tradition was first given by Avalokitesvara, known as the compassionate Buddha. Called the Great Mantra, it is considered the highest expression of the flow of love from the heart—the love that conquers even death itself.

Om Mani Padme Hum
Om Mani Padme Hum
Om Mani Padme Hum

It is written in the Śūrâgama Sūtra:

How sweetly mysterious is the transcendental sound of Avalokitesvara. It is the "primordial sound of the universe" (the pure Brahman sound). It is the subdued murmur of the sea-tide setting inward. Its mysterious sound brings liberation and peace to all sentient beings, who in their distress are calling for aid; it brings a sense of permanency to those who are truly seeking the attainment of *Nirvana's* peace.[1]

The meaning of the mantra is "O, thou jewel in the heart of the lotus." The jewel is the sacred fire. The jewel is the threefold flame. The jewel is the soul entering the threefold flame ensconced in the very secret chamber of the heart.

Milarepa, considered as one of the great masters of sound, is perhaps the foremost authority on the need for purity of heart. He said:

> If ye wonder whether evil *karma* can be neutralized or not, then know that it is neutralized by desire for goodness. . . .
>
> Without attuning body, speech, and mind unto the Doctrine, what gain is it to celebrate religious rites?
>
> If anger be unconquered by its antidote, what gain is it to meditate on patience?. . .
>
> Unless one meditate on loving others more than self, what gain is it merely from the lips to say, "Oh pity [sentient creatures]"?[2]

Padma Sambhava

Padma Sambhava is the great Guru of Tibetan Buddhism. His appearance in the eighth century was prompted by the pleas of King Indrabhuti to Avalokitesvara, who called in turn to Amitabha. Amitabha allowed an emanation of himself to strike the Lake Dhanakosha, and a

Tibetan tanka depicting Padma Sambhava (19th century)

lotus blossomed. A second emanation from his heart produced Padma Sambhava, the lotus-born one.

Padma traveled through many realms and worlds and became a master over the forces of nature; learned 360 languages, the lapidary arts, the inner, outer, and secret teachings of Buddhism, and ultimately he became a master of all existing knowledge.

During his travels, Padma Sambhava was challenged frequently by black magicians, whom he overcame often by pointing out the errors in his aggressor's doctrines. In the land of Zahor, when an enraged king sentenced him to be burned alive, Padma Sambhava transformed the pyre into a lake and appeared again as an eight-year-old boy.

About the middle of the eighth century, the king of Tibet asked Padma Sambhava to establish Buddhism in his country. When the priests, shamans, and demons of Tibet tried to destroy his work, Padma Sambhava defeated them. Instead of banishing the magicians, Padma made them take an oath to be guardians of the Dharma and made each a defender of a local town or province.

Gautama Buddha prophesied Padma's coming as one greater than himself, and foretold Padma's revelation of "the secret mantras to deliver all beings from misery."[3] Padma's teachings were conveyed to twenty-five disciples who are prophesied to return with his full message.

Padma Sambhava is very close to us. He carries the great love of Gautama and the great wisdom of the one who is the Guru, who is always willing to be God-taught. The great Guru will always be the chela of the greater Guru.

The Golden Mantra

Padma Sambhava's presence is felt as we intone his mantra, *Om Ah Hum Vajra Guru Padma Siddhi Hum.* Its meaning is "AUM. May immortal life be vouchsafed. Amen."

This mantra is a focal point of the unascended masters gathering their chelas to come to the feet of the ascended masters in the ascension flame. As you give it, you can feel the ascension flame of Padma unfolding as a lotus in your heart.

This particular mantra is to be used in the time of troubles when the Four Horsemen of the Apocalypse come forth with war, with disease and famine, death and hell.[4] All of these conditions are the planetary return of karma that must be transmuted by the sacred fire.

The action of this mantra is the establishment of a forcefield of light around you. It is like the establishment of the lotus flame as the ascension flame in which you abide. It is a secret-chamber, secret-ray action that ensconces your soul in the lotus within the tube of light. It carries the great peace of the Eastern mystics, of Lord Gautama, Lord of the World, of Lord Maitreya, and all of the many bodhisattvas who are pursuing the path of the Buddha and of the Mother.

The *Om Ah Hum* represents the threefold flame in the I AM Presence, the Christ Self, and in the heart. The *Vajra* is the earth-touching mudra celebrating Gautama Buddha's victory over the forces of evil and his claiming the earth as his proper place for the realization of samadhi, nirvana, enlightenment, and to bring back with him deliverance from suffering and the cause of suffering, which is wrong desire.

The *Guru* is the giving of the teaching. The *Padma* is the mighty balance of the figure-eight flow. The *Siddhi* is the fearlessness mudra of the turning back of all darkness. And the *Hum* is the balance once again in the center of the lotus of the heart.

> *Om Ah Hum Vajra Guru Padma Siddhi Hum.*
> *Om Ah Hum Vajra Guru Padma Siddhi Hum.*
> *Om Ah Hum Vajra Guru Padma Siddhi Hum.*

9

FUSION THROUGH LOVE

We have a mantra that was given to us by beloved Djwal Kul, the master of Tibet. It is for the release of the light of the heart. This is a meditation of the heart on the twelve solar hierarchies, which correspond to the twelve Hebrew sounds released through the name I AM THAT I AM—the twelve paths of initiation that lead to the center, the central sun of being.

Djwal Kul, the great Tibetan master, has served with the masters K.H. and M. in the Theosophical Society. He has given forth tremendous teachings on the present, the hour of the New Age, the hour of the community of the Holy Spirit, the mystery school—and he has delivered his "Intermediate Studies of the Human Aura."[1]

In that book he explains the use of this wonderful mantra. To me it represents the blending of East and West—the Eightfold Path of the Buddha, the Christic initiations of Jesus—the fusion of East/West, Father/Mother, Alpha and Omega.

We enter into the Word by the authority of the master whose mantra it is. And so we open the mantra with a call, the command to the master, "Djwal Kul, Come! In the center of the One," in the very heart chakra, anchor the radiant sun of thy heart. Be there the "magnet of the Threefold Flame."

This mantra has power because it was delivered by Djwal Kul as the very geometric pattern (the *yantra*) of the sound of his own inner heart. Through it he conveys his attainment to his disciples. As you approach it with love, the master approaches you with love.

There is a fusion of being, a fusion of spheres of consciousness. As you bow before his light and he bows before the light within you, there is a divine interchange. You lay upon the altar the untransmuted self, he lays upon the altar the spheres of his cosmic consciousness. He gives back to you the untransmuted self transmuted; you absorb his cosmic sound and light—and your gift to him must be a gift in world service.

DJWAL KUL, COME!

Djwal Kul, come!
In the center of the One,
Anchor now thy radiant sun,
Magnet of the threefold flame,
Expand God's aura in God's name!

Djwal Kul, come!
Threefold fountain, fill my heart;
Let thy angel now impart
The name of God—I AM THAT I AM,
I AM THAT I AM, I AM THAT I AM,
   I AM THAT I AM!

Djwal Kul, come!
Flame of gold, pink, blue, and white,
Seal thy victory star of light;
Renew my vows to God's own name;
Come, O Christ, in me now reign!

Djwal Kul, come!
Expand the fire of the Sun;
Alpha 'n Omega, make us one,
Seal my energies in Christ,
Raise my energies in light!

Djwal Kul, come!
Align my consciousness with thee,
Make us one, O make me free!
Seal my heart and hand in thine,
In God's mind I AM divine!

Djwal Kul, come!
Blaze the action of the Whole,
With light of victory fill my soul;
Return me to the Flaming One,
I AM begotten of the Son!

Coda: I AM God Power, I AM God Love,
       I AM THAT I AM, I AM THAT I AM,
          I AM THAT I AM!

       I AM God Mastery and God Control,
       I AM THAT I AM—
       AUM [chant]
       I AM THAT I AM—
       AUM [chant]

       I AM God Obedience now,
       To thy Law I vow,
       I AM THAT I AM, I AM THAT I AM,
          I AM THAT I AM!

       God Wisdom flame I AM,
       God Wisdom flame I AM,
       God Wisdom flame I AM!
       AUM—God Har-mo-ny [chant]
       AUM—God Har-mo-ny [chant]
       AUM—God Har-mo-ny! [chant]

       God Gratitude, God Gratitude, God Gratitude!
       I AM God Justice in full view,
       I AM God Justice in full view,
       I AM God Justice in full view!

       God Re-al-i-ty! [chant]
       I AM God Vision, God Victory won,
       I AM God Vision, God Victory won,
       I AM God Vision, God Victory won!

The Passageway
to Higher Consciousness

One of the great spiritual and democratic leaders of all times, Mahatma Gandhi, echoed the beliefs of the sages when he said:

> Mantras bring solace to those entangled in the meshes of worldly attachment. Let every individual depend on the Mantra which may have given him peace. For those, however, who have known no peace, and who are in search of it, the name of Rama can certainly work wonders.

> God is said to possess a thousand Names; it means His Names are infinite; His glory is infinite. That is how God transcends both His Names and Glory. The support of the Name, however, is absolutely necessary for people so long as they are tied to their bodies.

> In the present age, even ignorant and unlettered people can take shelter under the monosyllabic Mantra. When pronounced, the word "Rama" makes a single sound, and, truly speaking there is no difference between the sacred syllable "OM" and the word "Rama."

> The glory of the Divine Name cannot be established through reasoning and intellect. It can be experienced only through reverence and faith.[2]

In reverence and faith, let us give our bhajan to Rama.

> Hare Krishna Hare Krishna
> Krishna Krishna Hare Hare
> Hare Rāma Hare Rāma
> Rāma Rāma Hare Hare

The devotion that we pour to the Cosmic Christ through the name of Rama centers in the heart as love, becomes a magnet in the heart that raises all of one's energies. And as you develop a momentum on this form of devotion, the kundalini (the sacred fire) rises from the base to the crown, and you find that the energies become centered in the third eye.

There is peace, integration, alignment in the four lower vehicles. The soul is free to pass through the passageway into higher dimensions of consciousness. And from that focal point of light, the issuing of the dynamic decree, the command of the Word for the altering of human conditions, becomes of maximum power because one is seated in the very lotus throne of one's own Christ Self and I AM Presence.

10

THE BURNING BUSH

The creative power of the Word is understood in the Hebrew tradition and was greatly revered in the esoteric teachings of the Kabbalah and ancient Near East.

There are twelve names of God that come forth from the Kabbalah—the body of esoteric Hebrew teachings that explains and harmonizes the relation between God and his creation. These twelve names release the light of the twelve hierarchies of the Sun, twelve manifestations of God, twelve points of God-realization.

Hebrew and Sanskrit are two languages that convey to us most accurately the inner light, which is the alchemical key to the transformation of the Word. We approach, then, the sacred name.

There are many names for God. Each time we pronounce the sacred name, a portion of God is experienced, and if we have intense love, adoration of God, we also will become that portion.

It is written throughout scripture, "Whosoever shall call upon the name of the Lord will be saved."[1] That which is saved is that portion of you that has become one with God through the recitation of the Word.

Hebrew Names of God

Ein Sof [chanted]*

Ein Sof

Ein Sof

This name conveys the experience of God without end—without end in a spherical sense. It is equivalent to Brahman, the Absolute, the Source from which emanates all of creation—the soundless sound, the Sun behind the sun, God that is Be-ness without attribute.

Ehyeh

Ehyeh

Ehyeh

The name of Keter means "the crown," the representative of the manifested spiritual substance of the Absolute. We move from the Absolute to an attribute, the manifested spiritual substance, the first emanation of the Absolute. It has a meaning of "hidden, not yet revealed, but coming forth from."

---

*For your fullest experience of the creative Word, we invite you to give these and other chants and mantras in this book aloud as you read.

Yah
Yah
Yah

The name of Hokhmah, the second emanation, vibrates at the plane of God's cosmic intelligence.

Yehovah
Yehovah
Yehovah

The name of Binah, the third emanation, the plane of divine wisdom.

Eloah
Eloah
Eloah

The name of Hesed, the emanation of grace and mercy.

Elohim
Elohim
Elohim

The name of Gevurah, the fifth emanation, the plane of justice, judgment and the fear of the LORD.

Yehovah
Yehovah
Yehovah

The name of Tiferet, the sixth emanation, the plane of beauty and compassion.

Yehovah Tzevaot
Yehovah Tzevaot
Yehovah Tzevaot

The name of Netzah, the seventh emanation, the plane of victory and constancy.

Elohim Tzevaot
Elohim Tzevaot
Elohim Tzevaot

The name of the eighth emanation, Hod, the plane of glory and majesty.

El Hai
El Hai
El Hai

The name of the ninth emanation, Yesod, the plane of foundation or justice.

Adonai
Adonai
Adonai

The name of Malkhut, the tenth emanation, the plane of kingdom, royalty, the plane of Shekhinah, the divine immanence.

Ehyeh Asher Ehyeh
Ehyeh Asher Ehyeh
Ehyeh Asher Ehyeh

I AM THAT I AM. The name of God revealed after he brought forth the creation.

	ATTRIBUTE	NAME
Ein Sof	God without Attribute	Ein Sof
Keter	Crown	Ehyeh
Hokhmah	Intelligence	Yah
Binah	Wisdom	Yehovah
Hesed	Grace, Mercy	Eloah
Gevurah	Justice, Judgment, Fear of the LORD	Elohim
Tiferet	Beauty, Compassion	Yehovah
Netzah	Victory, Constancy	Yehovah Tzevaot
Hod	Glory, Majesty	Elohim Tzevaot
Yesod	Foundation, Justice	El Hai
Malkhut	Kingdom, Royalty, Shekhinah, the Divine Immanence	Adonai
I AM THAT I AM	The Name of God Revealed to Moses	Ehyeh Asher Ehyeh

Hebrew Names of God

There are twelve archangels ensouling these sounds. As we chant them, the vibration of the consonants and the vowels carries us to the heart of that God and to the heart of the hierarchies who adore that sacred name. Out of this sound and these syllables comes forth the entire manifestation of their cosmic consciousness. Out of these individual words, endless spheres of cosmic consciousness are manifest. These are like the Sanskrit seed syllables.

These words are in the esoteric tradition, the inner path of the esoteric Hebrew teachings. The exoteric path is what is contained in the outer scriptures of both the Old and New Testaments. The exoteric knowledge is the outer knowledge that can be taught intellectually. But the esoteric tradition can be conveyed only heart to heart, by the chain of hierarchy of the Word. You can purchase many books on the Kabbalah. You can master it academically. But to become the syllables, you must enter into the Word—the Word incarnate.

Moses and the Word

In the book of Exodus, we read that an angel of the LORD appeared to Moses in a flame of fire out of the midst of the bush that burned but was not consumed.[2]

As Moses was contemplating this phenomenon of Spirit-Matter science, the LORD called him aside,

Moses before the Burning Bush, Domenico Fetti (c. 1616)

appeared to him, and gave to him the great commission of going forth into Egypt to rescue the children of the light from their oppressors. It was a great commission, one that could not be accomplished without the Word incarnate in Moses.

If you have any ideas about rescuing the children of the light on earth, remember that it cannot be done without the Word. And this is why we are gathered under our tent to commune in the same Word who is "I AM," who initiated Moses.

Moses said unto this God who appeared to him:

> Behold, when I come unto the children of Israel,
> and shall say unto them, "The God of your fathers
> hath sent me unto you," and they shall say to me,
> "What is his name?" what shall I say unto them?[3]

Moses was highly educated. He knew all of the traditions of the Egyptian priesthood. He was brought up in Pharaoh's court. He knew the meaning of the sacred name. He was inquiring of this God, "What is that sacred name that is the key to going forth into Egypt to do those things which you have told me to do?"

This was no idle question. Moses knew that his entire mission hinged upon that Word that was with God in the beginning and upon the name of that Word which would be the light to unlock the sacred fire that would deliver the children of Israel from the power elite of Egypt.

Their power was not small; but it was entirely misqualified power—the misuse or inversion of the name of God, which is black magic. These intonations I have given you are pronounced backwards by the fallen ones in a fallen language of the fallen angels. This misused power presents itself as the anti-power of the power of God. It cannot be dealt with by a mere academic knowledge of the Word. It can only be dealt with by the transfer of the Word from the hierarch of the Word to you.

This is what was happening to Moses—the encounter with the LORD who embodied the Word.

> And God said unto Moses, "I AM THAT I AM."
>
> And he said, "Thus shalt thou say unto the children of Israel, 'I AM hath sent me unto you.'"
>
> And God said moreover unto Moses, "Thus shalt thou say unto the children of Israel, the LORD God of your fathers, the God of Abraham, the God of Isaac, and the God of Jacob, hath sent me unto you.
>
> "This is my name forever, and this is my memorial unto all generations."[4]

The memorial is unto you. You are the generations who have descended from the hierarchs Abraham, Isaac, and Jacob if the Spirit of the LORD and the seed of light dwell in you.

Moses and the Burning Bush, Sébastien Bourdon (17th century)

The name belongs to you. The name I AM THAT I AM is your birthright. It is the culmination of the quintessence of man's conception of God, which God gives to us through the Great Guru, Sanat Kumara.

Sanat Kumara is, was, and forever shall be unto us the incarnation of this Word. Sanat Kumara figures as the great archetype of light, as the Father principle in the major texts of the world's religions East and West. He is known by many names. In the Bible, Daniel saw him as the Ancient of Days. Karttikeya is one such name in the Indian tradition. And Sanat Kumara actually has certain texts that were written by his disciples of conversations of his teachings to them concerning the sacred Word.

It was Sanat Kumara, the Ancient of Days, who appeared to Moses and transferred to him this name, this vibration.

Nothing Changes without the Incarnation of the Word

Moses therefore becomes the incarnation, which means the embodiment, of this Word. Because he embodies the Word, he embodies the Lord behind the Word, the master who has embodied it before him. Hence, he becomes the incarnation not only of the vibration of the Word but the Person of the Word, who is Sanat Kumara. This is Moses' anointing as Guru of the twelve tribes of Israel.

Without that Guru—which means "God incarnate" —they cannot be liberated by the power of the Word. The Word must be with them because without the Word is not anything made that was made. Nothing can be done in Egypt without the Word. Nothing can be done in the United States of America without the Word. Nothing will move, nothing will change.

You can travel around the world to places you

have been ten, twenty, thirty years ago; you can meet people that you knew then. Without the Word nothing changes. Atoms, molecules, electrons, vibrations, records of death, records of war, records of hate and hate creation on the planet do not move. And generation upon generation the people continue to embody those vibrations that are the perversion of the Word.

Only the Word can undo the perversion of the Word. The Word, then, is a light. The Word is a sound. The Word is a person who has embodied both.

This is something that many people who pursue the science of mantra omit. They recognize there is an energy in the repetition of mantras, so they would take the mantra without the cause behind the effect. There is some gain in the repetition whether of Sanskrit or English or Hebrew mantras. But there is not the putting on of the garment of the Lord, the identification with the Person of the Word.

We all need the Guru. We all need Sanat Kumara. And we find Sanat Kumara embodying these twelve manifestations, these twelve words of God, the first being God without attribute. Therefore, coming forth from him are all of the rays of the sons of God who have embodied, many of whom are now ascended masters. All of the vibrations of cosmic expression are contained within him.

Moses, then, is receiving his anointing. I give it to you with the full weight of the experience so that it can be crystallized as a blueprint within you, as something that you determine to seek and find, so that it becomes the goal of your path to enter into this communion with Sanat Kumara.

There are many, many ways on that path that you must walk until you come to that full experience of the incarnate Word. It is not something that suddenly comes upon you in a moment because you attend a seminar. It is the very goal of your life, and there are many requirements including the balancing of a large percentage of karma.

The Real Self and the Lesser Self

Moses saw that sacred fire, that permanent portion of himself. It was the Presence of I AM. And this Presence, shown as the upper figure in the Chart of Your Divine Self, is the focal point of our meditation because this is the goal of our being. By that meditation we draw forth the Word to work the works of God.

Until you have the attainment and the grace of God upon you with the fullness of the presence of the Person of the Word, you have an advocate with the Father in the person of your Christ Self, the middle figure in the Chart.

Your Christ Self is the Word incarnate. Therefore, already present with you is the Real Self, the anointed Self, the Christed Self. By the authority of that Christ Self, you then speak the Word before the hour of your attainment, before the hour of your soul's fusion with the Word.

When you speak in that form, "In the name of my beloved Christ Self, I call the I AM THAT I AM . . . " and you direct the light of God into the conditions of the matter universe, it bypasses the densities of your own form, your vehicles, the skeins of consciousness. Whatever your lack of attainment, it does not matter. You are bypassing the absence of God that you have yet to transmute. And the clear, crystal water of Life of the I AM Presence comes through the Christ Self and performs the perfect work of the Word.

Always remember with greatest humility and reverence, that even as you speak it is not you, the lesser self, speaking, but it is God in you that is the doer and the speaker. When you make the mistake of saying, *I* have called upon the name of the LORD, *I* have done this, *I* have changed the weather, *I* have healed the sick, *I* have done this, *I* have done that, you are diminishing the power of the Word within you as you speak.

The desire to take the Word and to put your name and your fame upon it is the certain defeat of your path

The Chart of Your Divine Self

of evolution. The human ego, the carnal mind that is yet present in the untransmuted self would like to take the glory for the works of God. It cannot be. And therefore we always say, "Glory to the I AM THAT I AM. Praise the LORD and only praise the LORD."

To be an instrument of the great doer and to retain individuality is one of the great mysteries of the Path. It is a razor's edge where we have a firm sense of our identity and yet at the very moment of the firm sense of identity, we know that there is only one Supreme Identity, and that is God with us, the Immanuel of Isaiah.[5]

The Great Mystery of the Holy Grail

This Immanuel, this Word, can interpenetrate matter. And the great mystery of the Holy Grail is that Spirit as the infinite sacred fire can penetrate finite matter. The fire can be in the bush. The bush is not consumed by it, is not overwhelmed by it, because the very atoms of the bush are at the same vibration as the sacred fire.

It is the eternal lesson that God can be the sacred fire, the all-consuming fire, where you are, here and now, and not destroy the finite self in the state of becoming, because the seed atom of your being contains in its nucleus that sacred fire, and therefore you are not destroyed— even though the very fire is the consuming fire.

Moses exclaimed in the very face of this sacred fire, "Our God is a consuming fire."[6] Yet the bush is not consumed. When you invoke the consuming fire of God where you are, you fear not. That which is consumed is that which is unlike God. It is the understanding that energy as Spirit, as the masculine thrust of a cosmos, descends and interpenetrates the feminine polarity, the Matter bowl of being.

God reveals himself first as principle, as energy, as fire. The first glimpse Moses has is the pure sacred fire. The object is the translation of what he sees to himself. I AM the bush that burns but is not consumed— self-awareness. You can see the vision of the bush, and all of a sudden you see it as a cosmic grid. Passing through it is the sacred fire.

When you close your eyes and meditate, you visualize the grid. The sacred fire passes through it. Identity is being fired at the same time that it is being transmuted, accelerated, and elevated. The fire is the thread of contact with the Great White Brotherhood, with all souls throughout cosmos who are Real.

The sounding of the Word releases the sacred fire. It is sealed tight in the seed atom, as tight as fire is sealed in the nucleus of a physical atom. It cannot be probed or opened without the sounding of the Word. And the Word must be sounded with love. Love is a heat.

Love as an adoring sacred fire approaches the sealed permanent atom. And it is love and love alone that causes it to be opened and the release of sacred fire upon you.

You can intellectually repeat mantras or dynamic decrees, and the stream you receive is minute. You can enter into the joy of the LORD and feel so much love for God that you are fairly bursting with the love. And the love burns as a fire in your heart until it almost becomes a pain because the heart cannot contain so much love.

Then you open your mouth and intone the word and recite the prayer, and it is no longer a trickle but a torrent, a Niagara of light, because you have succeeded in prying open the seed atom, and the joy and the glory of the LORD is upon you by love.

Principle and Person

First the energy and the principle. Then the person embodying these steps through the veil and talks with Moses face-to-face. When you first begin to intone the Word, you will receive light, energy, principle, consciousness. When there is an equivalency of the Word within you as you walk this path, one day there will stand before you the ascended master who embodies the same light that you have invoked and become.

Today the ascended masters are standing before us and in our midst. The raising of physical sight to be one with the inner third eye becomes then the tangible experience that was had by Moses. You should look forward to it, anticipate it, but be nonattached and nonpossessive.

If you are attached and possessive, you will find imposters of that Word coming to you as discarnates, disembodied spirits, and masters of the false hierarchy. They are waiting to pose as the person of Jesus Christ, the Holy Spirit, El Morya, or Saint Germain. They go to those who anticipate the presence and person of God and demand it before they have become it. If you do this you will have your reward, but the reward will be the lesser manifestation.

The problem with these psychic beings is that they are tenacious in their energy and powerful in their magnetism. They bring strong delusion. They are mayic in emanation.

They are easy to contact because you do not have to change your vibration to contact them. And so they are the imposters of the ascended masters. Many are satisfied with the imposters, just as many are satisfied with the fallen angels in government and in the economy. You have to determine what level of the Word you are seeking and then realize that there are disciplines and initiations on the Path in order to attain to that level.

God is a god of love. His love manifests as the security of knowing that no one can pass to the plane of the Holy of holies unless his vibration be pure. Therefore we are secure in that law, that the Word itself cannot be tampered with. It can be imitated. It can be betrayed. It can be perverted in black magic ceremonies. But none of these endure.

And so, if you are the real disciples of the living Word of our Lord Sanat Kumara, you will pursue your path with patience, you will run and not be weary.[7]

Esoteric and Exoteric Law

Although God had given the Israelites access to his name, their lust for power and for the flesh culminated in Moses breaking the tablets on which the Law was written.

He fasted forty days on the mountaintop where the LORD told him he would worship—the very mountaintop of the vibration of I AM THAT I AM. He came down. He found that Aaron had allowed them to build a golden calf, and they were dancing and exhibiting the lusts of the flesh.

The first tablets that Moses brought down from Mount Sinai contained esoteric truths. The breaking of

Moses Breaking the Tablets of the Law, Rembrandt (1659)

those tablets was the breaking of the esoteric tradition conveyed to the children of Israel.

Moses returned to the mountaintop and received a second set of tablets, which were a set of exoteric laws —laws of dos and don'ts—because a rebellious people must live under such laws. When they would become the embodiment of the exoteric law by obedience to the simple Ten Commandments, then once again they could be given the esoteric tradition.

The name of God then became an anathema to the children of Israel because it brought to them the instantaneous return of their personal karma. Merely to speak the name I AM THAT I AM means we are invoking the person of God to abide in this temple. When we invoke the name and we invoke the Presence of God, and the I AM THAT I AM descends through the Christ Self, it does not leave us at it finds us.

God built this temple to inhabit it. He will have it as he desires it. So it came to pass that although God vouchsafed this name as a memorial to all generations,[8] the people left off using it. Even the priests no longer spoke the name within the Holy of holies.

The Word is self-transforming. It will not leave you as it finds you. This is why people look for substitutes. This is why they will say a lesser vibration of the Word such as Lord or Adonai. It demands less of those who say it than the original Word—which brings the judgment to that which is unreal.

But the children of Israel were attached to unreality and all that they enjoyed in Egypt. They did not want to leave it behind. They wanted a guru who would allow them to keep everything they enjoyed of the human consciousness *and* give them the light of the Word.

People want God's help, but they want him to help them within the context and the framework of their own human consciousness. So they say to God, "Deliver us from our pains, our diseases, our famine, our inconveniences, our wars, but don't take from us the pleasures we enjoy and the things we want to keep."

We want to be human beings, but we want God to deliver us from our plight. But God says, "I want you to be God. I want you to be perfect as I am perfect. And this is the condition of my impartation of the Word."

When you accept the condition, you find that everything you think you are surrendering is returned to you, but it is returned transformed. You give God all of your old consciousness, all of the things stored in the attic, all of the junk in the basement, and he gives back to you the jewels of light, of his divine attributes—energy for energy.

It becomes so very difficult to part with those things of the lesser self, but when we take courage and we do, we enter into a new life of the Spirit. Our joy is full. Our cup runneth over.[9] There is nothing that we ever had in the world that we do not now have in its transformed and purified and joyous state. And what's more, the things that God gives to us are the things that we get to keep.

Our souls are clothed upon with the white garment that is the blending of all of God's gifts of consciousness. When God comes to deliver, he really delivers.

Transformation by the Word

And so I am here to deliver not my word, but his Word to those who are willing to follow it where it will take them, to be transformed by it, and who fear the LORD in a sense of awe, who have the courage and the desire to become one with him through the science of the spoken Word.

It takes courage and a sense of self-worth to say, "LORD, I will be where you are. I will understand that holy ground is where I stand because thou art the I AM THAT I AM where I am. I will live accordingly." You are responsible for every use of the Word that you make, even in your daily conversation and in all that you think or say or do, all that you feel, because all of this is one level or another of the Word itself.

I am saying this to you to give you a reverence for life in the midst of a civilization that is losing its sense of reverence for life. We find that in the United States today, taking the name of God in vain is in vogue. Blasphemies, words that invoke only darkness, are a common part of everyday conversation. We can scarcely go anywhere and not hear this blasphemy of the Word.

People feel good when they say these words because it is an action of their own ego interacting with discarnates, who do give them a form of energy. It is a low-grade energy like an electrical current. And so in the absence of the repetition of the sacred name, which the people rejected because of the responsibility it puts upon them, they began reciting the names of lesser vibrations.

YOD HE VAU HE (YHVH) is a four-letter word. So is *Word.* So is *LORD,* which stands for Jehovah, which is simply the addition of vowels to the *YHVH.*

YHVH in ancient and modern Hebrew script

YHVH is a name of God found in the original Hebrew text of Exodus 3:15. The term is often translated in English as LORD (with the ORD in small capitals). Ancient Hebrew texts only include consonants, and no one knows how the word was originally pronounced. Jehovah and Yahweh are two forms that have been proposed, with the former being more widespread historically and the latter preferred by most modern scholars.

God gave us his name as the name wherewith we are saved. Yet at the rate that people are repeating these four-letter words, you would think that they were their very salvation.

When you have a reverence for God and the Word, these things matter. They begin to hurt you because God himself is disgraced each time they are spoken. So Joshua said, "Come apart and be a separate people."[10]

That is only the beginning of absence of reverence for life. There are many, many manifestations of this in our society today, culminating in murder itself, but going through all of the degrading vibrations that we hear in advertising, see on billboards, and on and on and on, that are misuses of the Word itself to program the people around a status quo of materialism instead of to exalt them to the I AM Presence.

The descent through the misuse of the Word builds and builds and builds until you are in the greatest darkness and density. But all of this can be undone, as the ascended masters have taught us. The Hebrew names of God are exalting. They immediately elevate the soul to the point of the I AM THAT I AM. It is not a long, involved process. It can happen easily and quickly.

11

THE AVATAR

In Christian cosmogony, the Logos or Word through whom the world was created became flesh, and it was manifest in and as Jesus Christ. How is this different from the transfer of the Word to Moses?

Moses simply had a greater portion of karma than Jesus did when he embodied. Moses killed an Egyptian in his anger,[1] and therefore he had to reincarnate. He had a final incarnation in China before he ascended, as Jesus Christ ascended. It is a question of degrees, of how much the Word or Logos, how much God is actually integrated with the flesh form.

In Jesus Christ, as in no other, we find the perfect integration of the Word, so he is supremely called the Word incarnate. But we must not allow ourselves to feel that the incarnation of the Word is not approachable by ourselves. We would walk in his footsteps, and we would do so because he has allowed it, willed it, ordained it. "And the Word was made flesh, and dwelt among us (and we beheld his glory, the glory as of the only begotten of the Father), full of grace and truth."[2]

The most exalted concept in all of religion and philosophy is this incarnation of the Word—the flame burning in the bowl of being. In the Sanskrit language, the word for Logos becoming flesh is *avatara*. And so there have been numerous great avatars who have directed the course of history.

The avatar is understood to be the perfect self-presentation of God in his Son, the perfect manifestation of the Word embodied in a form, in a person, in a physical body that we can see. And because we can see it, we can follow it back to the Source and become it ourselves.

When you say, "In the beginning was the Word," you are there in the beginning, you are there in the fiery core of your I AM Presence. You're not sitting in an exoteric sense with your outer mind repeating a few words. That is not the science of the spoken Word. It is loving the vibration, going with it, stilling the outer self, and being able to equate with God.

The Son of God Is Where You Are

It is written of Jesus that he "thought it not robbery to make himself equal with God."[3] It is not robbery because God gives of himself to us liberally. Don't allow the wolves in sheep's clothing to tell you that it is blasphemy to affirm that the Son of God is where you are. And that God *is* where you are, and that the mighty I AM Presence, the Christ Self, *is* God with you—Immanuel. Do not allow these fallen ones to take from you your birthright.

You can go nowhere without the Word, and the Word is God's memorial to you—the generations of his light and his seed. This is the white-fire core teaching of the Great White Brotherhood and the foundation of the science of the spoken Word. The Word is the power of God, the activating, creative force. This is the force with us that Isaiah named as the Immanuel. *Immanuel* means "God with us," God incarnate as Christ.

This Christ I declare to you to be your real created, uncreated Self—created because God created it as his image and likeness in whom all things are made; uncreated because you yourself have not yet re-created his matrix, his pattern to fashion your own identity out of its image and likeness. You could not create anything that was not already created. The Real Self is created, is perfect in its spiritual house, temple, and vibration. The mighty work of the ages of your soul is to re-create that Self where you are.

Each time you intone the Word, a portion of your

Real Self is created in the Matter universe and God comes into this temple. That is what our daily dynamic decrees are all about. Through the correct use of the Word, identification with the Word, men and women have freed their souls from the rounds of rebirth to follow the conquerors of death and hell who have gone before them on the path of soul liberation by the Word.

God's Attributes

It is apparent that Indian philosophy has influenced Hellenic, Semitic, and even Egyptian thought to some degree. However, there are some differences between the Christian idea of *Logos* and the Indian concept of *Vak*—the Word.

Hindu theology actually considers the Word to be the Mother of the Trinity of Brahma, Vishnu, and Shiva—the Creator, the Preserver, and the Destroyer. This philosophy then places the Word with God, above and beyond Father, Son, and Holy Spirit—the Trinity of Christian theology. We can understand this when we remember that the definition of Brahman is God without attribute.

As soon as we say God *the Father,* we have a manifestation of God with attribute. We have a person we can visualize and identify. As soon as we say God *the Son,* it is a personification, an attribute, and similarly for the Holy Spirit. Therefore, the Word with God in the beginning without whom was not anything made that was made becomes the means for the manifestation of God with attributes.

Ultimately, when you have the manifestation of the Trinity that is the threefold flame in your heart, that Trinity in turn creates and manifests, and we ourselves then become embodiments of the attributes of the Trinity. This places Mother or the sense of Mother, because Mother again becomes an attribute, behind the creation of the masculine forms of deity.

Father, Son, and Holy Spirit are ways of the Path that we walk in. People looking upon us should see one or more or all of these attributes manifesting from time to time. All of us must manifest Father Person from time to time to other parts of life, the Son Person, the Holy Spirit—Father as the Lawgiver, as the authority of the Law and the defender of the Law; Son as the embodiment of wisdom and the teachings; Spirit, of love and comfort. All of these are continually flowing through us as the light emanations of the Trinity.

In Indian thought, then, we adjust our minds to consider that the Word as Vak is the supreme shakti or the potent power, yet it is one with Brahman. On the surface, this unification of the Word in God appears at odds with theological Christianity, but a deeper view of both Hindu and Christian cosmogony reveals the fundamental supremacy of the Word of God.

The Incarnation of the Word

In Hinduism, the incarnation of the Word is held to be with all men and can be directly known and developed as the soul seeks to become united with it. This is the Hindu conception of the soul as *jiva,* that element of being that is in the process of becoming God through his Word.

All of the sons of God are light emanations of the Guru Sanat Kumara. As Moses was initiated by Sanat Kumara, he foreknew the coming of the Word incarnate in Jesus Christ. And he spent his entire mission preparing the children of Israel for the coming of the Word as that Saviour who is able to transfer the light of the threefold flame as an initiatic rite to those that believe on him as the Word incarnate.

The meaning of believing on the name of Jesus Christ is to believe that he is an avatar, an incarnation of the Word, and a very specific incarnation—the one assigned to you and to me. We don't simply go prancing around the universe picking gurus. Gurus pick us. Jesus said: "You have not chosen me, but I have chosen you."[4]

The Avatar of the Age of Pisces

We find a great rebellion in the world today in America and in all nations—bypassing this incarnate Word for other teachers, rabbis, masters, great writers, great prophets. They have all come. But Jesus Christ is the initiator, not only of the Piscean age, but of the age of Pisces as an initiatic cycle within our own being.

We all have to pass through the age of Pisces in our own soul development. We're moving into Aquarius in a planetary sense. But in a personal sense, some people have never gotten through the age of Taurus or the age of Aries.

Each age has its avatar. If you missed the last one, you have to take the one who is with us now and through that one go back and pick up the dropped stitches of the previous avatars.

Moses, then, is preparing the children of Israel to receive that Word incarnate. Prophets foresaw his coming, the esoteric Jews in their traditions were preparing for his coming. The very few returned to Jerusalem from captivity when given the opportunity to do so, to be there in the hour when his birth was predicted.

Jesus, then, has become the stumbling block for many who cannot get past this conception, this mystery of the Holy Grail that is so important, the sacred fire burning in the bush, but the bush not consumed.

Therefore we find that the ascended master Saint Germain as that Word incarnate is every whit as much the initiator of souls with the true light that lighteth every man, because the only begotten Son of God manifests itself over and over and over again wherever there is the fullness of the incarnation. Words of the Christ: "If it were not so, I would have told you."[5]

If it were not so, you would not have a divine identity as the Christ Self. There is only one Son in infinity. As soon as infinity manifests in the finite, it must repeat itself because we have dimensions of time and space. The bush is repeated over and over and over again. Suddenly you see on the screen of your mind a million bushes blazing with the sacred fire and a million souls blazing with the one only begotten Son of God.

Why are you not God-realized? Because you have feared to understand that he led us to this co-equality with God. He "thought it not robbery to make himself equal with God." God has created you, sons and daughters of light, to be co-creators with him.

What does it mean to co-create? It means that the outline of the self on the backdrop of God's being is just that, an outline. Here is an outline drawn on the screen of life. It is really God, God with an outline that has form and consciousness.

Take a piece of paper. Make a model of yourself. In your mind you can do this. And you look at it, and you hold up the piece of paper, and you realize that you are really the paper. The paper is God. You are merely an outline.

You have to have the mystery by the sense of the flow of the Word. The bush is not separate from the sacred fire. The bush of itself does nothing. With the sacred fire, it becomes a co-creator with God. "Moses, go and be a co-creator with me." That is the message of Sanat Kumara.

We always understand ourselves as servants of the light, instruments of the I AM that is declared. Where I am God is speaking the I AM. It is not the lesser self laying claim to that I AM. That would be the point of idolatry.

The Office of Saviour

The office of Saviour was realized to its fullest potential in Jesus Christ. We see an expression of Saviour in Moses, but the full and total, complete manifestation of the Saviour is here in Jesus. Who is our Saviour? Our Saviour is the LORD God Almighty manifest in the person of Sanat Kumara. And Sanat Kumara manifests in his sons.

When Jesus began his mission, he went into the

temple, he picked up the scriptures, and he read from the Book of Isaiah. He defined his mission as follows:

> The Spirit of the Lord is upon me, because he hath anointed me to preach the gospel to the poor; he hath sent me to heal the brokenhearted, to preach deliverance to the captives, and recovering of sight to the blind, to set at liberty them that are bruised, to preach the acceptable year of the Lord.[6]

This is what the Saviour, your own Christ Self, is speaking at inner levels.* When the triangle of your being becomes congruent with the triangle of your personal Saviour—your Christ Self who is your Saviour through Jesus Christ, through Sanat Kumara—then the oneness of these two triangles becoming the six-pointed star of David in your heart enables you to say the very same Word with the very same vibration that Jesus spoke it two thousand years ago.

In the hour of Jesus' baptism there is a declaration of the incarnate Word. The dove descends out of heaven and the voice of God declares: "This is my beloved Son, in whom I AM well pleased,"[7] meaning "in whom I AM in manifestation."

In the hour of the transfiguration, there is again the testimony: "This is my beloved Son, in whom I AM well pleased; hear ye him."[8] Listen to his Word.

—————————————
*And you can affirm it aloud right now.

Transfiguration of Jesus,
Carl Bloch (c. 1865)

He is the Word; he is the messenger of the Word—the twofold office in one.

That was the message of the transfiguration, but Peter, James, and John were in the idolatrous sense. Immediately they wanted to erect three tabernacles to commemorate the ascended masters whom they saw —Moses, Elias, and Jesus.

But the Word of God to them is, "Hear ye him." He is the Word and he is the tabernacle of the Word. You have no need to build the tabernacle when you have the Word with you.

"Hear ye him." Hear him now as he speaks in the very chamber of your heart. The Transfiguring Affirmations of Jesus Christ come from this mountaintop experience.

TRANSFIGURING AFFIRMATIONS OF JESUS THE CHRIST

I AM THAT I AM

I AM the open door which no man can shut

I AM the light which lighteth every man
    that cometh into the world

I AM the Way

I AM the Truth

I AM the Life

I AM the Resurrection

> I AM the Ascension in the light
> I AM the fulfillment of all my needs
>   and requirements of the hour
> I AM abundant supply poured out upon all life
> I AM perfect sight and hearing
> I AM the manifest perfection of being
> I AM the illimitable light of God
>   made manifest everywhere
> I AM the light of the Holy of Holies
> I AM a son of God
> I AM the light in the holy mountain of God

The affirmation of these statements that Jesus gave to his disciples is another way of affirming your identity. When you say, "I AM," you are saying, "Where I AM, there God is; and where God is, there I AM."

Only God living in you can speak the name I AM with authority. And when he speaks it, there is an exploding and an imploding of light from the fires of the very heart of the Central Sun. And each time you say the name of God and enter into that consciousness, you are one with God.

As you do this daily, you become more and more real until you come to that point where you feel such total identification with God that you can truly say, "I AM God in action here," and truly feel that he is one with you.

It's as if God were a great cloud of white fire, and this cloud is moving toward you more and more each time you say "I AM."

All of a sudden, you are congruent with that cloud. You are in the center of it and you can't find yourself anymore, because you are one with this cloud and the self becomes one with the mist that is God. The drop becomes one with the ocean.

12

SCIENTIFIC PRAYER

We have been speaking of the offices of Christ, of his declaration of his mission, quoting from the Book of Isaiah announcing the acceptable year of the Lord—the Lord's incarnation, the Lord Sanat Kumara within him. We spoke of his self-declaration as messenger. We speak now of his declaration as the Word.

By the transfer of the Word of the Son of God, by the arcing of the light of the heart, by the initiation of the heart of Sanat Kumara, the avatar has the power to make the children of God Sons of God.[1] God himself is not a materialist. God himself can perform this mystery.

Jesus said, "The night cometh when no man can work. As long as I am in world, I am the light of the world."[2] The night that was coming was the night when he would no longer be in this octave. And in order for him to be in this octave again, we would have to come to the place of the Second Advent, when Christ is born and dwells within *our* temple.

He is the light of the world again when we allow the full occupation of our temple by Jesus Christ—the Christ Self of each of us and ultimately every ascended master. And so our temple becomes the habitation of the Lord and the Lord's representative, whoever that representative may be.

The Thread of Contact

Jesus well understood the traditions of the ancient teachings of the Vedas, the Upanishads. All that is taught in Hinduism he was aware of.* He came in the long lineage of avatars of East and West sponsored by Sanat Kumara.

The transfer of the light of the Ancient of Days through Moses to the children of Israel and then again through Jesus illustrates the thread of contact. To transfer the law of the sacred fire was the purpose of his coming. And he was the unbroken thread of contact with Mount Sinai, the Holy of holies where God revealed himself.

Therefore, the power to transfer the Word and the works continues as Jesus promises that not only will we do the works that he does, but whatsoever we ask in his name, that he will do, that the Father may be glorified in the Son.[3]

---

*Ancient Buddhist manuscripts speak of the years Jesus spent in India preparing for his Palestinian mission. See Elizabeth Clare Prophet, *The Lost Years of Jesus*.

The Word is the person of the Guru who overshadows us. This overshadowing is accomplished as we invoke the Electronic Presence of Jesus Christ. The Electronic Presence is his God-identity, his cosmic consciousness, his auric forcefield. Wherever you are, if you have the right relationship to him in love, which is the foundation of your prayer, you may say, "In the name of the Lord Christ who abides in my temple, I invoke the Electronic Presence of Jesus Christ where I stand."

When you can instill in yourself the love of meditating on beloved Jesus, and realize that it is for this purpose that he lives; when you can totally identify with his reality and your heart becomes a magnet for his heart, then Jesus will stand where you stand. He will place his sacred heart over your heart. His sacred heart becomes a Great Central Sun magnet that magnetizes your own heart flame to expand and be pulsating one with his heart.

This is a very important call, and it gives you the beginning of the sense that you are truly one with the saints in heaven. You are a part of the entire Spirit of the Great White Brotherhood. As an unascended chela you can be one with any ascended master, and then you can identify with the promise, "The works that I do shall ye do also, because I go unto my father."[4]

Jesus in the mighty I AM Presence places his Presence over you. You therefore have a multiplier of the Word that is already in you. The Christ in you multiplied by the Christ of Jesus produces the greater works. And this gives us the understanding of this mystery that we must expect to realize in this hour.

The law of self-transcendence, of an ever-expanding cosmos, of God transcending himself hour by hour means that Jesus Christ today is no longer Jesus Christ as he was at the age of thirty or thirty-three. In two thousand years, the expansion of his Cosmic Christ consciousness is even beyond our comprehension. Therefore, let the multiplier of the Word be upon you.

We must remember, "Jesus, the Christ," and then speak your own name, "_____ , the Christ." And therefore, realize that Jesus was the Son of man who came to embody the Son of God. This is your mission also. And his mission is not fulfilled until we proclaim this living Word. Our authority to pray comes from the Lord himself. The great Word incarnate is the giver of the Word.

Respect for the Word

I have given you these teachings to establish the sense of the holiness of the Word that is given to us, that we not take for granted the dynamic decree, the meditation, the prayer, the fiat, the affirmation; that we realize that mantras do not work merely because they are scientific formulas of sound. They work because they are transferred to us—the living God unto his living sons and daughters.

Jesus came to earth to restore to us the lost Word—lost because it was misused and abused for thousands of years. He returned to us the power of the Word that Moses received from Sanat Kumara and sought to give to the children of Israel, but they would not. They did not continue in his Word I AM THAT I AM. And therefore Moses' mission is fulfilled in Jesus Christ. But it is only fulfilled in us if we accept the lineage of the hierarchy.

Jesus was very particular about prayer. He said, "It is the spirit that quickeneth: and the flesh profiteth nothing."[5] The words of a mantra without the Word incarnate are vain repetition. He said:

> And when thou prayest, thou shalt not be as the hypocrites are: for they love to pray standing in the synagogues and in the corners of the streets, that they may be seen of men. Verily I say unto you, they have their reward [the admiration of men who watch them standing in the streets].
>
> But when thou prayest, enter into thy closet [the secret chamber of the heart], and when thou

hast shut thy door, pray to thy Father which is in secret; and thy Father which seeth in secret shall reward thee openly.

But when ye pray, use not vain repetitions, as the heathen do: for they think that they shall be heard for their much speaking.[6]

We must not approach the living Word with vanity and the desire for self-glory but with respect for its supreme and sacred science. "The words that I speak unto you, they are spirit, and they are life."[7]

Seven Commands

Jesus was very specific in teaching his disciples how to pray. He taught them to enter the closet—to go into that point of contact with the I AM Presence—and then he proceeded to give what has been repeated in the glory of his light countless millions of times by Christians for two thousand years—the Lord's Prayer. This is his transfer of the authority of the Word.

Jesus taught the repetition of the Word, just as its science has been practiced in the East for thousands of years. He taught this yoga of the Word, giving adoration to the Person of the Word. And he warned against its vain and blasphemous misuse.

We know that the seven mighty Elohim brought forth the entire Matter universe by the spoken Word.

They responded to the self-creative fiat of the Word "Let there be light: and there was light." And the seven days of Creation are the seven cosmic cycles for the lowering of the light of God from the plane of Spirit to the plane of Matter.

When Jesus gave to us his Lord's Prayer, he gave one form of the prayer in the exoteric or outer tradition, and he gave the second form in the esoteric or inner tradition. It is a question of levels of initiation. So I will begin with the one that is familiar, that is in the Bible.

Both of these commemorate the seven spheres of Creation, so that each time the prayer is given, there is a lowering into manifestation of the fullness of your causal body, there is an alignment of the seven chakras, there is the re-creative power-wisdom-love of the Word manifest in you.

Jesus said, "After this manner therefore pray ye."[8] He was giving the form of prayer, the code, the seven steps of precipitation. He was also telling us what Isaiah has told us—the point of the command, the commanding of the Word, the commanding of the energy of God by the authority of the Word transferred to us through the Guru.[9]

He opens the prayer with the address to the Father, which is the address to the mighty I AM Presence in the Person of Father.

Our Father who art in heaven,

Beloved I AM Presence who art in the sphere of my cosmic consciousness. By this repetition of his Word, we create an arc of energy from our heart to our Christ Self, to the source of light. The moment we speak, there is a descent of light. The adoration goes up and the return current creates the closed circuit. The address is always necessary in any form of prayer.

There follow seven commands. They are not requests. They are spoken in the imperative mode. They follow the seven color rays that come forth out of the white light of the Holy Spirit. And they mark the seven paths of our initiation toward our own personal Christhood and incarnation of the Word. The first one is

Hallowed be thy name.

By the authority of the Word, I am commanding the light in my heart and all being and consciousness everywhere to hallow the name of God, I AM THAT I AM. I am saying that the crystal clear stream of God descending from the mighty I AM Presence now has impressed upon it reverence for the name of God. It's an invitation for the great sphere of my own God consciousness to manifest here below as above.

This is the first command on the first ray of the will

of God. It corresponds to my throat chakra and to the color blue, which is the power of God. This prayer is the prayer of sons of God who are co-creators with the Father.

The second command is the second ray. It corresponds to the crown chakra. It is a very simple command. When spoken with authority, it moves heaven and earth.

Thy kingdom come.

Wherever *kingdom* is written in the New Testament, it is translated esoterically as consciousness. It means, "Thy consciousness come." In each of these commands, we are exercising a freewill choice. We are saying that we prefer the unlimited consciousness of the mind of God to our own limited intellect. Therefore, on the second ray the mind of Christ descends to become congruent with our own mind. The very command in itself displaces the anti-mind.

The third command is the third ray of the pink flame of love, and it centers in the heart.

Thy will be done on earth, as it is in heaven.

Our devotion to the will of God is a matter of intense love, not fear of punishment. By love I am choosing to be obedient to the will of God, to ensoul it, to become it. I am accepting it unequivocally. It is a commitment.

It is a surrendering of this temple and this life to be the embodiment of God's will—not as a robot, not as a puppet to God, but as a conscious inter-actor moving with the mind of God, discoursing with him, understanding the reason, the Logos of God, and drawing God-solutions to the problems of earth. When we surrender to that will, God fills our temple and we move forward in the attainment of his God consciousness of love.

There is only one way that God's will is going to be done on earth, and that's through you. Don't look around at anyone else. Through you the will of God will be done on earth as it is in heaven. And you are responsible for your point of reality.

The fourth command follows the fourth ray, the white light of the ascension, of the purity of the Mother, the white light of the base-of-the-spine chakra—the very foundation of life in Matter.

Give us this day our daily bread.

It is wonderful to know that we have this rela-tionship to God and that God as Mother provides for us the abundant supply, the abundant life, all that we need including the bread on our table, including enough money to pay our taxes and give God our tithe and pursue spiritual paths and do good for others.

When we can give this command, we have an intimate relationship with God. This Son who is intimate with the Father commands the transfer of his rightful inheritance. This is a freewill choice that this moving stream of energy will be stamped by the fourth ray with every need and requirement of the hour.

The fifth command is on the fifth ray. The vibration of it is green. It corresponds to the third eye. It is science, truth, and precipitation. There is no science without the law that Jesus is giving us here. This is the law that is the foundation of the science of the flow of supply and demand. It is the law of forgiveness.

And forgive us our debts,
as we forgive our debtors.

We cannot stand in the Presence of our Christ Self if we have withheld forgiveness from any part of life. Even if you don't remember that you failed to forgive, it still is there as that thing that divides you from your God. Therefore, we do not hate, because our hatred binds us to the object of our hatred and separates us from our own Christ Self.

We can't command life, we can't command energy unless we are a part of the Christ in all of us. As we resolve with one another, God resolves with us. And we find ourselves in the state of oneness whereby we can precipitate abundance.

The sixth command corresponds to the sixth ray of service and ministration, the purple and gold ray. It anchors in the desire body through the solar plexus.

And lead us not into temptation.

The temptation is to be someone else than your Self, to be your not-self. The temptation is to be someone else, to covet someone else's life, to be the unreal self.

That command invokes the guardian action of God so that the desire body will be held firm in the desire of God. God is in us right now desiring to be God. Every moment God is pulsating within your desire body desiring to fulfill himself through you.

Every billboard, every television show, every movie, almost everything that our senses contact is some kind of a focal point to get us away from the original desire to be God and the fullness of God, to be something else, to look like this or that, to dress like this or that, to eat this or that kind of food that's being advertised—to do all kinds of things that distract us from that point.

The seventh command comes under the seventh ray, the violet ray, and it is anchored in the soul, the seat of the soul.

But deliver us from evil.

We're crying out, deliver us from this evil, this energy *veil* we've created. God has a way out. We invoke the Holy Spirit. It strips from God's energy our overlay, our misqualifications.

"Lead us not into temptation" falls under the sixth ray of the Piscean age. Jesus came to show us who we should be—the living Christ. And he showed us all of the temptations that would beset us to take us from that path—from persecution to mockery, to everything else that we see portrayed in the gospels that surrounded him.

"Deliver us from evil" is the sign of Saint Germain and the Aquarian age, that we have the courage to stand before God with all of the karma that we have made for thousands of years and say to him, "Deliver us from evil."

"Why, the audacity!"—that is the consciousness of the carnal mind. It would tell you that you have no right to ask God to take from you that entire momentum of karma.

But God has the answer—he gives the science of the spoken Word, he freely dispenses the violet flame, and day by day he puts us to work, he gets us to recite the Word, and he says, "If you will work and recite the Word, I will deliver you from all of your karma so that you can ascend Home free. You can balance 100 percent of your karma. You can return to me in this life because I have accelerated my Word by the Holy Spirit."

It's exciting that this dispensation of the Lord's Prayer anticipated the hour of the Aquarian age when we would be delivered from this karma. Finally, the eighth statement:

For thine is the kingdom and the power
and the glory for ever. Amen.

This is the sealing of your alchemy, the sealing of the seven steps of your precipitation. If we're going to take God's energy and create with it, we must give acknowledgment. "Thine is the kingdom"—"God, it's your consciousness, your energy, your power, your glory for ever whereby this work of the Word is done through me. I of mine own self can do nothing."

And then we say, Amen, AUM. The sealing of the prayer seals the fiats we have made in a sphere of light. They are cast into the cosmic ocean, and the very commands working out in the seven spheres return to us the answer. And of the Son of God, the Lord has said, "My word shall not return unto me void."[10] It shall accomplish the thing whereto I have sent it.

Let us chant the outer, or exoteric version, of the Lord's Prayer together.

THE LORD'S PRAYER

Our Father who art in heaven,
Hallowed be thy name.
Thy kingdom come.
Thy will be done on earth as it is in heaven.
Give us this day our daily bread.
And forgive us our debts as we forgive our debtors.
And lead us not into temptation
But deliver us from evil.
For thine is the kingdom and the power
and the glory for ever. Amen.

Immense joy comes upon us when we realize that we can pray this prayer as Jesus prayed it, as the command unto the Word that was with God in the beginning. This is a command that must be fulfilled by cosmic law. It must be answered.

However, when you send forth the call, if you have a momentum of absence of forgiveness as density in your world, the answer comes back as mighty light rays, but those light rays do not instantaneously fulfill these specific commands. They come and begin to bombard the density with which you have surrounded yourself by disobedience to God's laws, perhaps in ignorance.

With the breaking down of that substance, there is a chemicalization in your forcefield. Sometimes it is very uncomfortable. Sometimes it produces a physical heat. And sometimes you cry out against the living God because of the burdens that come upon you, because the light forces you to balance your karma.

So we have the mantras of Saint Germain, the forgiveness mantra and the violet flame, which will help you to daily transmute the density so when you give these commands, you can see the evidence of their greater and more immediate manifestation.

The I AM Lord's Prayer

Jesus gave us the exoteric version of this prayer in the imperative mode because the command itself is intended to raise the soul to the position of authority. Even if the soul does not understand why it has the authority to command the light of God, the prayer itself will take you there.

Now as we advance on the path of Christhood, we realize we have gone through the stage of the command. These commands have manifested within us. We know the God who lives in our temple; we know the I AM Presence. We are now with Jesus in the Upper Room, and he gives us the I AM Lord's Prayer, affirming that all that we have commanded is now come into manifestation where we are.

THE I AM LORD'S PRAYER

Our Father who art in heaven,
Hallowed be thy name, I AM.
I AM thy kingdom come
I AM thy will being done
I AM on earth even as I AM in heaven
I AM giving this day daily bread to all
I AM forgiving all life this day even as
I AM also all life forgiving me
I AM leading all men away from temptation
I AM delivering all men from every evil condition
I AM the kingdom
I AM the power and
I AM the glory of God in eternal,
     immortal manifestation—
All this I AM.

When you say, "I AM," you are saying, "God in me is." When you are one with God, there is no separation. The I AM of God speaking is the only I AM of you because you have surrendered all lesser identity. The identity of God where I AM is the identity you have claimed.

The two prayers are very different: one represents the Alpha and the other the Omega of consciousness. Because we have been giving Jesus' Lord's Prayer as beggars for so long, it's important that we take the inheritance of giving the I AM Lord's Prayer as joint heirs with the Lord Christ who taught it to us.

And do you know, as it says, "All this I AM"— I can experience the Word that I AM two thousand years from now or ten million years ago. I can experience myself into the future in ascended octaves of light and tell you exactly what I AM doing. That is the power of the Word of the mantra, the repetition of this Word.

And why is it so powerful? Not because anyone sat down and wrote a prayer—no, because someone by the name of Jesus Christ said this prayer, spoke it on the ethers—spoke the outer prayer to the outer multitudes, the inner prayer in the Upper Room—and both were recorded. "Heaven and earth may pass away but my Word shall not pass away."[11]

The Word he spoke as though it were spoken freshly from his mouth is being pronounced in this very room in this very moment—the fresh words of your Guru spoken in the inner ear impressing you with crystal fire, letters of living fire, putting the engram on the tiniest atom, on the very seed of your being.

The I AM Lord's Prayer is the Word of God, who was with him in the beginning. It is the Word that is life. As you accept this mantra, as you give it daily, it will transform you. You have free will. You're the scientist in the laboratory. You're the soul becoming. So it's up to you. God has given you every gift.

There have been saints who antedate the incarnation of Jesus Christ by thousands, tens of thousands, hundreds of thousands, and millions of years, to become ascended masters, cosmic beings, Solar Logoi, sponsors of systems of worlds, planetary systems—one and all are the Word incarnate. If you desire their light, you must accept them personally.

There is one Guru, the Great Guru, God, who sent Sanat Kumara, who in turn sponsored the lifewaves of earth and other planets. We have but one Guru, yet we acknowledge the ascended masters as the living gurus. We are not divided or compromised, nor is Jesus Christ compromised, when we go to the heart of Saint Germain, acknowledging him as the Word, giving our love to his person, and accepting his Word as the mantra of being.

Thus, you take what I have said in terms of love, adoration, honor, worship of one Son of God and you see that the worship is of the Word—the Word itself that is the Sun behind the sun of the personality. We worship God in the ascended masters. We worship God wherever God is manifest. That is the Hindu tradition.

You can multiply the teachings we have given this day, apply them to each and every one of the ascended masters, and discover new spheres of consciousness. They are not jealous of one another; they do not vie for positions in hierarchy as the fallen angels do. The ascended masters are a mosaic of cosmic harmony, each one contributing their momentum of service and dedication and their own yoga.

Mantras of Saint Germain

Whatever is the requirement of your soul, you begin to use the mantras of the ascended master who most fits your life, your calling, and what you are desiring to do in that particular moment. We are going to explore their mantras, their decrees, and what they specifically do for us.

We've taken the mantras of Jesus for our initiations under the hierarchy of Pisces. Now let us take the mantra of Saint Germain for our initiations under the hierarchy of Aquarius. Saint Germain has many mantras, and he suggested we use this mantra for the healing of the economy.

I AM THE LIGHT OF THE HEART

I AM the light of the heart
Shining in the darkness of being
And changing all into the golden treasury
Of the mind of Christ.

> I AM projecting my love
> Out into the world
> To erase all errors
> And to break down all barriers.
>
> I AM the power of Infinite Love,
> Amplifying itself
> Until it is victorious,
> World without end!

For each and every one of the ascended masters there is a very special personal experience. Some people tell me that on this or that occasion through the teachings of the ascended masters they suddenly came to understand as they have never understood before their personal relationship to Jesus or to Saint Germain or to Gautama.

It is a moment of quickening (which could be called conversion), when something leaps in your heart simultaneously as it leaps in the heart of the master. There is a fusion of your being with his. You have an intense love for him. And ever thereafter, the mantras of that particular master have a deep and personal meaning for you.

I remember when I first saw the picture of Saint Germain. I was about to leave for college. I saw his face, and I felt his flame leap into my being. It was an instantaneous recognition of the Guru who is the hierarch of the Aquarian age, the very personal master who was embodied as Saint Joseph and the prophet Samuel.

The more you know about the master in his previous incarnations, the more you know about his teaching in the present by the Holy Spirit, the more you are part of him, the more he is part of you.[12] You begin to learn how his mind works, how he thinks, how he would react to certain conditions of life on earth and what

The Ascended Master Saint Germain

he would do about them. And you love him so much that you go out and do what he would do because you know that the one thing he doesn't have in this octave is a physical body.

The ascended masters have everything else, but they don't have hands and feet and hearts that beat and mouths that speak and can convey their teaching. So we develop a very intense compassion for our elder brothers and sisters on the Path, for all that they would do and all the light that they have, they cannot do unless we open all the stops and let them work through us.

Saint Germain releases his intense action of the violet flame through his "I AM the Violet Flame" mantra.

I AM THE VIOLET FLAME

I AM the violet flame
  In action in me now
I AM the violet flame
  To light alone I bow
I AM the violet flame
  In mighty Cosmic Power
I AM the light of God
  Shining every hour
I AM the violet flame
  Blazing like a sun
I AM God's sacred power
  Freeing every one

Raising the Planet

The light of the Word that is in Saint Germain lives in you in this mantra, takes over the mantra, recites it, accelerates it, steps up its vibration, and carries you with it.

The Word could be conceived of as being the Cosmic Christ consciousness, like a cosmic computer that takes a reading of the entire condition of our consciousness and our karma. The Word that is the foundation of the mantra knows exactly what we need in that mantra.

When I begin to say this mantra, without even thinking, the mantra goes faster and faster and takes me to a point in my being—the line between light and darkness—a certain position where that light swallows up the darkness in the world around me.

You all have a certain quotient of light in you, a certain amount of light that is your momentum through decrees or service or love or whatever you have done in all of your lifetimes. That point of light, which is your point of the Word, is the point where you give your mantra. And your mantra proceeds from that point to transmute the next levels of darkness you are facing.

As you transmute a layer of darkness, you occupy that space. It's like being in a battle. You've conquered that territory. Now it's yours. You're standing at a new level of light, and you have accelerated. You have new attainment from the experience. So as you give the mantra again and again, you are standing at different points of frequency and vibration.

You might like to start out giving this mantra very slowly, with devotion, which is perfectly all right. It's very powerful when it's done slowly. But as I step it up, it can accelerate to the point where it becomes almost indistinguishable as individual words. You only hear a tone because that is where my cosmic consciousness is at work manifesting the works of God.

When we come together in unison, we try to reach a middle ground. But it's nice sometimes for you to be able to hear what happens when you do transcend certain levels. The important thing to remember is that the Word itself decrees the tempo. You need to tune in to the Word at the heart of the mantra. And there are occasions when a very intense momentum is definitely right at the point where the light is consuming vast quantities of human effluvia over the cities of the earth.

When you can sit and give mantras for an hour and clean up an entire city, it's because the Word of God in you has reached a tremendous acceleration and a moment that has become a momentum. It's something to strive for and it's something to watch.

There is a tremendous release of light in the acceleration of the Word by the heart of God, by the

Presence of the Word. And when you think about the many people around the world who are keeping that tempo in their homes, you can realize that there is an arcing of the light and the sound ray from city to city and nation to nation, and the angelic hosts descend. They multiply your mantras, and they expand them, and they use them for the raising of the entire planet.

So what the Great White Brotherhood has given to us in these dynamic decrees is a great power. It is the power of their causal bodies. Every master has many concentric spheres of light. They focus these through you for world service when you give these invocations.

Kuthumi and I AM Light

Many of you are lovers of Saint Francis. We know him as Kuthumi. In his book *The Human Aura,* he teaches you how to visualize yourself going into the heart and focusing there.[13]

I received a letter from someone who told me that the first ascended master he came in contact with was beloved Kuthumi through this book. He picked up the book, read it, gave the mantra, and from the moment of the first giving of the mantra, he knew he was free from marijuana and would never smoke marijuana again.

It was the person of Kuthumi through the Word, through the mantra, that gave to him that healing—and

The Ascended Master Kuthumi

it is a healing, because there are very intense forces connected with marijuana. When you realize the power of the Word in one ascended master and one mantra given once to break that binding spell and all that goes with it, you must realize that the hosts of heaven are able to meet every problem that we face.

As we give this, let us visualize what we are saying

intensely happening where we are. See yourself sending an intense beacon of light from your heart out from this city to every city in America, raising consciousness for the specific solving of our complex problems.

Make contact with the heart of Saint Francis. Get to know him and realize that this is Kuthumi. And make one request of him—a habit or a problem that you may have—maybe the way you do or don't do something or something that has you in its grips—and ask him to deliver you from it.

We can always be healed of something, no matter how far we go on the Path. And by this prayer and communion, you may enter into a closer relationship with this ascended master, who was very close to Jesus. Together they occupy the office of World Teachers, busy night and day, as it were, giving intense instruction to those who are lovers of the wisdom of God and to all people who need the teachings of Christ.

And so you say, "In the name of the Father, the Son, the Holy Spirit and the Mother, I decree:"

I AM LIGHT

I AM light, glowing light,
Radiating light, intensified light.
God consumes my darkness,
Transmuting it into light.

This day I AM a focus of the Central Sun.
Flowing through me is a crystal river,
A living fountain of light
That can never be qualified
By human thought and feeling.
I AM an outpost of the Divine.
Such darkness as has used me is swallowed up
By the mighty river of light which I AM.

I AM, I AM, I AM light;
I live, I live, I live in light.
I AM light's fullest dimension;
I AM light's purest intention.
I AM light, light, light
Flooding the world everywhere I move,
Blessing, strengthening, and conveying
The purpose of the kingdom of heaven.

The issues that so challenge and beset us and seem hopeless give way to this intense moving stream of light.

Every mantra has a formula of the Word designed by the Word incarnate who sends it forth to consume by the sacred fire all that would impinge itself against the inner purpose of the mantra. This mantra has a purpose. It is for light to swallow up and replace darkness where darkness has been in your life.

As you begin to give the mantra, it becomes a series of initiations each time you speak it. Each time you speak it, the light will descend and actually be a ray that goes right after the opposite condition—it activates doubt that is opposing faith, or hatred that opposes love. So whatever you are seeking to have manifest, its anti-self or its antithesis is first aroused by the light. It gets stirred up because it has to be stirred up. It will come to the surface and be transmuted by the very mantra itself.

So in the first round of giving it you may feel the surfacing of momentums of doubt: "It really can't happen. It really can't be." The second time you give the mantra, you already feel it beginning to consume the doubt. And the third time, it's getting a rolling momentum. It rides right over the doubt, and it's singing with its own inner song of faith.

The mantra always works, but you have to work with it and move with it and recognize that whatever you want to change is a condition of discord in your life. That discord is going to scream loudly the moment before it goes into the flame and is no more. But if when it screams loudly, you give up and stop giving your mantra, then it's won the day and you're going to have to come back another day and give the mantra all over again.

The displacing of darkness by light is always a miniature Armageddon within your own world. And if you understand the nature of the science, you press on and you finish it. And when you feel things coming up from your subconscious, rejoice because the end of that condition is nigh. The power of the Word is greater than all that assails it. The Word will prove it to you if you let it.

This process becomes very exciting when every day at a certain hour you return to the Word of the mantra or a group of mantras that you have determined to ensoul and embody. And you watch how there are steps and stages of development of your cosmic consciousness and how that consciousness is always reflective of the master whose mantras you have chosen.

The Acceleration of Light

Sometimes we sing our mantras and sometimes we repeat them. When they are repeated with rapidity, there is a corresponding acceleration of light. A more intense pressure of light can be put through your heart chakra by Kuthumi when you speak with a loud voice. When Jesus raised Lazarus from the dead, he cried out with a loud voice. He didn't speak it softly. And the loud voice was the intense command, "Lazarus come forth,"[14] with a very intense action of the Word that compelled the threefold flame in his heart to reignite, the soul to return to the body, and the body to come out from the tomb—all of that by those three words, "Lazarus, come forth."

These mantras are commands. They are intended to be given aloud with a firm and determined commanding voice. Before that voice of God in you, the demons fear and tremble. They actually tremble before the sound of your voice, and they flee. They want to flee before the archangels come to bind them in bundles and cast them into the lake of fire.[15]

The Light of the God Star

We have a mantra to a being of light who has been known for as long as earth has existed and beyond, a cosmic being by the name of Surya. His seat of authority is in the star Sirius—which is called the Dog Star, but we call it the God Star.

Surya is very much involved with the Lord Jesus Christ in the judgment of the fallen angels. And he has promised to place his Electronic Presence wherever you are and wherever the fallen angels are on the entire face of the earth. He can multiply his body millions of times. You can visualize this mighty being Surya anywhere and everywhere on the face of the earth. And you can visualize him seated in the lotus posture as a mighty Buddha of light.

An Indian depiction of Surya as the Sun God

I'm going to make an invocation to Surya and then we're going to sing his song. While you sing, it is natural to pour love out to the being you are singing to, and when you pour that love, you are instantly with that being wherever he is. Whatever he is doing, you participate in it, and you benefit from his cosmic consciousness, which he transfers to you as you embody his Word, his works, his service.

INVOCATION TO SURYA

In the name of the I AM THAT I AM, I invoke the Electronic Presence of beloved mighty Surya over this company of lightbearers. Beloved Surya, I call for the millions of years of momentum of service to the light of the will of God that is within your heart to amplify God's will within us. I call for your Electronic Presence to come now into our life by the power of the Word.

Surya, judge that which is unreal within us. Bind it and remove it from us that we may pursue the path of our Christhood with all due haste and thereby assist in the liberation of the children of light on this planet. Fearlessly in love we invoke thy being where we are, Surya. Come with thy compassion and gentleness, and teach us to pray as thou wouldst have us pray.

In the name of the Father, the Son, and the Holy Spirit, we send thee, Surya, into the very midst of the dark and nefarious activities of the fallen angels upon this planet for the judgment of their councils of war, for the binding of war, the hordes of war, the plans of war. May one and all be cast into the lake of fire that the children of the light might go free. In the name of the entire Spirit of the Great White Brotherhood, Amen.

BELOVED SURYA*

1. Out from the Sun flow thy dazzling bright
   Blue-flame ribbons of flashing diamond light!
   Serene and pure is thy love,
   Holy radiance from God above!

Refrain: Come, come, come, Surya dear,
   By thy flame dissolve all fear;
   Give to each one security
   In the bonds of purity;
   Flash and flash thy flame through me,
   Make and keep me ever free!

2. Surya dear, beloved one
   From the mighty Central Sun,
   In God's name to thee we call:
   Take dominion over all!

3. Out from the heart of God you come,
   Serving to make us now all one—
   Wisdom and honor do you bring,
   Making the very soul to sing!

4. Surya dear, beloved one,
   From our faith then now is spun
   Victory's garment of invincible gold,
   Our soul's great triumph to ever uphold!

---

*May be given as a song or a decree

Because of the flame of harmony that is in a song, we find that we can immediately open ourselves, feel the love of the master, and pour our love to that master. The very harmony of the music puts us in a love vibration. That love and adoration for God is needed as the foundation for the giving of mantras. And there is so much more instantaneous power when you really feel that sense of love and devotion.

Then after you have sung it, you can take the very same decree and accelerate it with an intense power because the wisdom of God tells you that to accelerate this by love will release a far greater action of the causal body of the master.

God needs your energy and your light to manifest the solution to a problem. So you give his very own mantra back to the being whose Word you desire to have manifest. He's given you the mantra; you give it back to him by speaking it to him so many times in an evening. He takes the energy you send him, multiplies it by his causal body, and returns it to you as the solution.

It's a very exciting experience to feel the consciousness of a cosmic being when you are regular in your pursuit of that one. God cares about your very personal problems, those things that you think are so small that you don't even think they are worth writing him about or disturbing him about. He cares about them because they tie up your energy so you aren't free to use it for the bigger problems of life.

The expression of the spoken Word can vary from the singing of a song, which is the slowest form of the mantra, to the giving of a decree, to the invocation made by the spoken Word, all the way to the acceleration of this Word to the extent that you could scarcely understand it if the words were not in front of you.

This shows you the immense creativity possible in your own free expression of immersion in God's being, all of the different ways you can use the power and authority of the Word to approach God, to enter God's being, for him to enter your being, and for there to be an expansion of glorious light in dimensions undreamed of before.

LIBERATION THROUGH
THE WORD

One with God, directing the science of the spoken Word, we do not remain lost in the Himalayas. Looking down from that mountain of bliss, we are, with our Lord Gautama, intensely aware of human suffering, and therefore we direct the current of light into the very action of current events.

This is what the Coming Revolution in Higher Consciousness is all about. It is finding the peace that is not merely peace but that is the potential power behind the release of the Word. Going within in devotion is drawing back the arrow for the release of the spoken Word that is the power to create and re-create—to rearrange matter, molecules, consciousness, mind. This is the way to the solution of the problems that we face today. And so from this very high estate we come back to the ascended master decrees, and we call for the violet fire.

One of these decrees is a very dynamic call for the protection of our youth. Among our youth today are the avatars of the New Age. One would not think it possible for an avatar to lose his way, but it is possible. All of the avatars have required guardians and teachers. Many lightbearers are in situations where they are being programmed by schools and the media from such an early age that there is not the opportunity to realize the inner seed light in outer manifestation.

So when we come into the bliss of the Buddha, we then direct the light of the heart in a million intense rays,

The Ascended Master El Morya

infinite rays, to all the world for the protection of youth in every nation—for the protection of youth as the Buddha and the Christ and the Divine Mother and the reality within them. They scarcely have any teachers to point the way to the inner man of the heart, and they are only given the programming of the outer robot consciousness of mechanization and materialism.

All of us who have sensitivity to life are most concerned about the unborn, the little children, those growing up, that as precious flowers they have the proper environment to realize this immense light that they come with. And so our beloved El Morya, the ascended master, delivered to us this mantra. Most of you know him as Saint Thomas More. He said, I will write a short mantra so it will be given many times. Let's give it together.

PROTECT OUR YOUTH

Beloved heavenly Father!
Beloved heavenly Father!
Beloved heavenly Father!
Take command of our youth today
Blaze through them opportunity's ray
Release perfection's mighty power
Amplify cosmic intelligence each hour
Protect, defend their God-design
Intensify intent dIvine

> I AM, I AM, I AM
> The power of infinite light
> Blazing through our youth
> Releasing cosmic proof
> Acceptable and right
> The full power of cosmic light
> To every child and child-man
> In America and the world!
> Beloved I AM! Beloved I AM! Beloved I AM!

This can be given with the dynamism of the decree of that I AM THAT I AM. This is the tradition of the Guru Moses and Jesus Christ. It is the Western active principle that compels us to action and to strive for perfection in lowering into manifestation the inner blueprint and patterns of the cosmos.

So we follow the Eastern tradition of going within through the sacred AUM, going within in our devotion and love and our realization of beings upon beings of light who have realized God consciousness, hosts of the LORD, angels and archangels, unascended masters of the Himalayas. All of these come to view with the simple bhajan of Rama, the name of God as Gandhi said.

In that contact with millions of liberated souls by the light of the heart, we then return to our assignment in the world today. We turn to a dynamic decree, and when we give it in this powerful manner, all of the momentum of our love and all of our contact with the antahkarana of millions of souls pours through our heart as their love also goes out to the youth of the world.

The Silent Word Becomes the Spoken Word

This is why the science of the spoken Word is more than just an individual reciting a series of words. It's the means to contacting all sentient beings who have ever reunited with the Word—worlds without end. It's a very simple equation: Things equal to the same thing are equal to each other.

It's a principle of maximizing the Word. When you reach the point of light of the Word, you have reached the point of Creator in his creation. When you know you are there in meditation, the silent Word must become the spoken Word. It is our assignment in this Kali Yuga. All things must come now into manifestation —all of the inner spheres, all of the inner perfection.

This is the japa of the repetition of the Word. It has been taught for thousands of years. This very japa is the reason why we are here today, why there is a platform of planet Earth beneath our feet. Devotees in the East, in the Himalayas, since long before the sinking of Lemuria have sustained the spoken Word perpetually—day after day, year after year, century after century.

As long as there are some upon earth intoning the Word, there is the transfer of the light of the heart of successions of higher and higher planes of beings as the descending chain of hierarchy finally comes into manifestation in the keystone of the arch of being, which is you.

You are the keystone of the arch because you are positioned in the physical Matter universe, the most important position of all because this is the place to which all souls must return into incarnation to balance their karma. The plane where the karma is made is the plane to which souls must return.

The fallen ones have determined that souls will not return to this plane, that avatars will not be born. They have thought up all sorts of devices to see that this does not happen—a contrived energy crisis, a demand for zero population growth, the denial of life in so many different ways that we observe in our society.

Beyond all of the rationales that go with these, we find that the real reason behind the reason is to cut off the spiritual evolution of life and deprive the most transcendent beings from being on schedule in their incarnations upon earth—and so is the rationale behind the building up of nuclear armaments and the threatening of war. Mara and his armies are still there waiting to defy the one who will be Buddha.

Gautama Buddha gave to us a message that we have published in the book called *Quietly Comes the Buddha*. He teaches the path of Dipamkara and of the soul that is moving toward the center of the light of Buddha. The Ten Perfections of the Law give us an understanding that discipleship in the East is the other side of discipleship in the West.

With Christ and Buddha, we learn a twofold path that forms the planetary caduceus, the intertwining of the energies of Alpha and Omega. Both are necessary.

But we must not abandon our calling in the West. The West is where the battle is being waged. The West is where it will happen. The West is where the Saviouress is prophesied to come—the Saviouress as the Divine Mother who comes to deliver to us the understanding of the Word, and the Woman clothed with the Sun giving birth to the Divine Manchild as the Christ consciousness in all people.[1]

This is why our civilization, our youth, our people are under such intense bombardment of negative energies. The light that comes down with these beings of light stirs up layers and layers and layers of records of planetary karma, including the records that go all the way back to Atlantis. The records of Atlantis are with us in genetic engineering and in all sorts of inventions of science, both good and bad.

So here we are in the present reaping the past, the arbiters of the future. And there's only one way to make the future happen—by the freewill use of the science of the Word.

The Creative Use of the Word

The different ways that we are demonstrating show you how creative is the Word, how adaptable it is to your own nature and your preference as to the flow of that light and especially your need.

Saint Germain has stressed the violet flame as the action of the Holy Spirit that actually does transmute karma. It's the transmutation by the sacred fire.

The Apostle Paul by the Holy Spirit delivered to us a decree to the violet flame. It has a very special rhythm, and the rhythm of the mantra itself is a scientific pattern for the breaking up of recalcitrant substance surrounding the seven chakras of your being.

MORE VIOLET FIRE

Lovely God Presence, I AM in me,
Hear me now I do decree:
Bring to pass each blessing for which I call
Upon the Holy Christ Self of each and all.

Let violet fire of freedom roll
Round the world to make all whole;

Saturate the earth and its people, too,
With increasing Christ-radiance shining through.

I AM this action from God above,
Sustained by the hand of heaven's love,
Transmuting the causes of discord here,
Removing the cores so that none do fear.

I AM, I AM, I AM
The full power of freedom's love
Raising all earth to heaven above.
Violet fire now blazing bright,
In living beauty is God's own light

Which right now and forever
Sets the world, myself, and all life
Eternally free in ascended master perfection.
Almighty I AM! Almighty I AM! Almighty I AM!

The violet flame flows to the tempo of the heart, which is a three-quarter time. Freedom is the vibration of the seventh ray, the Aquarian age, and the violet flame. It frees up cells and atoms and electrons. It frees your consciousness, mind, and heart, and soul to be who you really are.

The Love of the Divine Mother

One of the great spiritual teachers of India of the nineteenth century was Sri Ramakrishna. By his

Ramakrishna (1836–1886)

absolute devotion to God as Mother and through austere yogic practices, he achieved great heights of divine awareness. He echoed Gandhi's admonition on the need for purity of heart in the science of the Word:

> Once you have developed a taste and rever-
> ence for the divine Name, you no longer require
> to exercise your faculty of reasoning or undertake
> any other form of spiritual discipline. All one's
> doubts are dispelled through the Name; the heart
> is also purified through the Name; nay, God Him-
> self is realized through the Name.[2]

Inasmuch as Ramakrishna was a devotee of the Mother, we would like to sing the bija mantras to the four goddesses who are the complements on the four cardinal points. We begin with Sarasvati, the counterpart of Brahma; then Laksmi, the counterpart of Vishnu; then Durga, the Shakti of Shiva; and finally Kali.

Om Aim Sarasvatye Namaha
Om Srim Laksmye Namaha
Om Dum Durgaye Namaha
Om Krim Kalikaye Namaha

Meditating upon the Divine Mother, we are struck by the great harmony of her love and her intense action for the protection of her children.

The higher we climb in consciousness, the greater the perspective we gain concerning the eternal truths of the divine Word. As we ascend to the top of a tall mountain, gazing out to the wide horizons that represent the flow of time, we can visualize many streams and rivers of vibrant self-returning currents leading to the ocean of God's being.

These rivers give off a certain harmonious vibration as they are the accumulated and ongoing effulgence of the chanting of God's name, of the sound of AUM, of Rama, of Krishna, of HUM. Flowing from the East, each person's stream of energy joins to form the mighty rivers of the return flow.

Think of how many times the mantra AUM has been chanted since the beginning of time. Undoubtedly, it is in the billions or trillions or even more. The river of AUM is wide and very strong, and we can instantly feel the momentum of devotees throughout the ages as we give this most sacred mantra.

As we proceed through the veils of time, we can benefit from all who have come before us. We jump into the river of the divine sound at its leading edge, and we are carried along with a momentum of this composite flow. As we study the metaphysics of sound and begin to apply what we learn, the power and practical efficacy of the Word will become very clear—crystal clear.

The Ascension Flame

In this day and age, the great synthesis and culmination of the science of the spoken Word has been brought forth by the ascended masters of the Great White Brotherhood. Throughout the decades, the masters have continually built a vast pyramid of understanding and practical techniques that utilize the Eastern knowledge, as well as adding many dimensions of the higher science including the safe raising of the Mother light in each one.

The Mother light is the ascension flame by which every Son of God is intended to return to the Source.

When you think of the Source as a great blazing sphere of cosmic consciousness, and the Mother light rising from the base unto the crown, you can feel yourself being buoyed up as on a jet of water, mighty in its power, until you are literally carried Home to the very center of God's being.

This is the ritual of the ascension that has been demonstrated by the avatars, notably Jesus Christ, Gautama Buddha, Zarathustra, Enoch, Elijah, John the Beloved, Mother Mary, and more recent saints such as Pope John the XXIII. The path of the ascension is the conclusion of the Eastern path of soul liberation.

This is the entire goal of the path of the ascended masters, the Coming Revolution in Higher Consciousness, and the reason you apply the science of the spoken Word. It is the union of your soul with Christ, and through that Christ, to the Word which was with God in the beginning.

In the beginning, we were with the Word in Brahman. We have gone forth to the farthest direction apart from that center of Be-ness, and we return to the undivided Word, to the Absolute—Brahman.

The Ultimate Return

This is the goal of all of our outgoings of evolution —the ultimate return. In this age, the ascended masters

have come to fetch us—not in UFOs and not by psychic phenomena. They have come because it is the
hour in the Kali Yuga when those who will use and
apply mantra yoga and the power of japa will discover
their reunion with the Word.

But reunion is not enough—for the Bride is not
received by the Lamb until that Bride has brought the
Word into manifestation for the healing of the world,
for the healing of the governments and the economies
of the nations.

So we walk parallel paths. As our souls soar back
to God, we are ever mindful to reach out to hold up
the little ones who need the thread of contact.

This thread of contact is the entire point of the
Great White Brotherhood. Every ascended master is
tied to every servant of God. If you can visualize this
contact heart to heart to heart about the universal
spheres, you get a picture of a massive skein of energy,
a grid, a forcefield of light, whereby we can chant the
universal AUM and understand its meaning:

We are one.

We are one.

We are one.

NOTES

CHAPTER 1 • Sound: Life's Integrating Phenomenon

1. John Woodroffe, *The Serpent Power: The Secrets of Tantric & Shaktic Yoga* (New York: Dover, 1974), p. 172.
2. Swami Pratyagatmananda Saraswati, *Japasūtram: The Science of Creative Sound* (Ganesh, 1972), p. 11.

CHAPTER 2 • Patterns of Creation

1. Hans Jenny, *Cymatics,* I & II, (Basel, Switzerland: Basilius Press AG, 1967 & 1974).

CHAPTER 5 • In the Beginning . . .

1. John Woodroffe, *The Garland of Letters: Studies in the Mantra-Sastra* (Madras, India: Ganesh & Co., 1979), p. 4.
2. John 1:1.
3. John 14:6; Rev. 3:8.
4. Gen. 1:3.
5. Genesis chapter 1 describes the original creation of man: "In his own image, . . . male and female created he them." This is the creation of the spiritual being of man, the higher vehicles. After the expulsion from Eden, chapter 3 says, "Unto Adam also and to his wife did the LORD God make coats of skins, and clothed them." The "coats of skins" are symbolical of the lower vehicles that were

necessary for the soul's evolution in the denser planes of matter.

CHAPTER 6 • **The Word in the Vedas**

1. Woodroffe, *The Garland of Letters*, p. 6.
2. Ibid., p. 7.
3. Ibid., p. 8.
4. Swami Sivananda, *Japa Yoga: A Comprehensive Treatise on Mantra-Sastra* (Shivanandanagar, India: Divine Life Society, 1978), p. 28.
5. F. Max Müller, trans., *The Upanishads* (New York: The Christian Literature Company, 1897), pp. 1–2.
6. Swami Nikhilananda, *The Principal Upanishads* (Mineola, N.Y.: Dover, 2003), p. 338.

CHAPTER 7 • **The Word, East and West**

1. Mark 1:40, 41.
2. Heb. 1:3.
3. Mark 4:39.
4. Agehananda Bharati, *The Tantric Tradition* (Garden City, N.Y.: Doubleday Anchor Books, 1970), pp. 19–20.

CHAPTER 8 • **Mantra in Buddhism**

1. Lama Anagarika Govinda, *Foundations of Tibetan Mysticism* (Boston: Weiser, 1969), p. 256.
2. W. Y. Evans-Wentz, ed., *Tibet's Great Yogi Milarepa: A Biography from the Tibetan* (London: Oxford University Press, 1969), pp. 253, 263, 264.
3. Tarthang Tulku, *Crystal Mirror*, vol. IV (Berkeley: Dharma Publishing, 1975), p. 3.
4. Rev. 6:1–8.

CHAPTER 9 • **Fusion through Love**

1. "Intermediate Studies of the Human Aura" is included in the *The Human Aura*, by Kuthumi and Djwal Kul.
2. Swami Sivananda, *Japa Yoga*, pp. 151–52.

CHAPTER 10 • **The Burning Bush**

1. Acts 2:21.
2. Exod. 3:2.
3. Exod. 3:13.
4. Exod. 3:14, 15.
5. Isa. 7:14.
6. Deut. 4:24; 9:3. See also Heb. 12:29.
7. Isa. 40:31.
8. Exod. 3:15.
9. Ps. 23:5.
10. Josh. 23:7.

CHAPTER 11 • **The Avatar**

1. Exod. 2:11, 12.
2. John 1:14.
3. Phil. 2:6.
4. John 15:16.
5. John 14:2.
6. Luke 4:18.
7. Matt. 3:17.
8. Matt. 17:6.

CHAPTER 12 • **Scientific Prayer**

1. John 1:12.
2. John 9:4, 5.
3. John 14:13.

4. John 14:12.
5. John 6:63.
6. Matt. 6:5–7.
7. John 6:63.
8. Matt. 6:9.
9. Isa. 45:11.
10. Isa. 55:11.
11. Matt. 24:35; Mark 13:31; Luke 21:33.
12. For information about Saint Germain's previous embodiments, see Mark L. Prophet and Elizabeth Clare Prophet, *Lords of the Seven Rays,* or Mark L. Prophet and Elizabeth Clare Prophet, *The Masters and Their Retreats.*
13. See Kuthumi and Djwal Kul, *The Human Aura.*
14. John 11:43.
15. Rev. 19:20.

CHAPTER 13 • Liberation through the Word

1. Rev. 12:1, 2.
2. Swami Sivananda, *Japa Yoga,* p. 152.

104 pp • ISBN 978-1-60988-367-6

The Law of Cycles
Finding Your Rhythmic Inner Peace

From early childhood, Elizabeth Clare Prophet observed the cyclic interaction of nature, planets and stars.

Drawing on sources ranging from Hindu teachings on pralaya cycles, the ancient Greeks' understanding of the golden ratio, to modern studies on the spirals of creation, she shows the rhythmic equation of God in man and nature. From this broad perspective, the wholeness and holiness of the universe are revealed.

Is it time to get off the roller coaster of the circumstances of your life and find your point of peace? Find your ultimate freedom through the mystery of the violet flame!

144 pp • ISBN 978-1-60988-398-0

Creative Thought Forms

The Art and Science of Spiritual Transformation

Mark Prophet, a modern-day adept, shows how you can use color, sound, and geometry to create thoughtforms that have a reality far beyond mere imagination.

Have you noticed how advertisers use thoughtforms to program your desires? How the news media use thoughtforms to program your mind?

There is real power in the science of thoughtforms. And this science can be used for many purposes—including the healing of mind and body. Thoughtforms can even precipitate in the physical plane. But of far greater value is their power to transform your mind and emotions.

How will you use thoughtforms to brighten your life, your mind and emotions with the balance, symmetry, and harmony of light?

112 pp • ISBN 978-0-922729-42-5

The Creative Power of Sound

Affirmations to Create, Heal and Transform

Recent scientific advances point to what mystics have
known for thousands of years: sound holds the key to the
creation of the universe—and it can create spiritual and
material change in our lives. Prayer is the sound and language of the soul. When spoken out loud, it can unlock the
dynamic energy of the spirit. In *The Creative Power of Sound*,
you will learn seven principles for applying prayers, mantras
and affirmations to your everyday life. You will discover an
effective way to harness spiritual energy to create positive
change for yourself and the world around you.

ABOUT
THE SUMMIT LIGHTHOUSE

The Summit Lighthouse is an internationally recognized spiritual center for the advancement of inner awakening. Our international organization is a global family that is inspired, guided, and sponsored by those known as the ascended masters.

The ascended masters are the most beloved and trusted transcendent beings guiding our planet's material and spiritual evolution. Most of the world's religions are currently based on the revelations of one or more of these masters before their ascension. We openly embrace spiritual seekers from all paths of light including the mystical traditions of the world's religions.

The ascended masters and their messengers have given us over fifteen thousand hours of invaluable inner wisdom and insightful instruction, and they have provided the means for our direct initiation into higher consciousness.

For the ascended masters . . . no subject is off limits! Their teachings contain amazing truths and awesome answers on spirituality, alchemy, astrology, sacred geometry, spiritual science, karma, reincarnation, ascension, archangels (and fallen angels), and even those issues that are considered taboo or "out of this world."

Primary Goals of the
Teachings of the Ascended Masters

The ascended masters challenge us daily to be bold, to dare to be who we truly are, and to face adversity with courage, patience, perseverance, honesty, integrity, inner love, discipline, and discernment—all for a greater sense of inner peace, fearlessness, stillness and silence, harmony, self-mastery, compassion, and wisdom.

These teachings help our souls get back to the origin of their individualized inner source of True Self Love— the Higher Self, or I AM Presence. Our point of contact with our Higher Self is the "Spark of Life" or "Sacred Fire of the Heart," the place where our consciousness expresses its true divine nature of unconditional love and happiness, universal oneness, and an authentic desire to serve others.

How Our Teachings Came into Being

Our teachings were all released through highly trained and trusted messengers, Mark L. Prophet and Elizabeth Clare Prophet. Mark was contacted by the Ascended Master El Morya at the age of eighteen and received training from him for many years before he was instructed to establish The Summit Lighthouse in 1958 in Washington, D.C.

With his ascension in 1973, Mark passed the torch for the mission to his gifted wife, Elizabeth Clare Prophet, who continued her service until her retirement in 1999.

The dictations of the ascended masters were regularly given in public. The ascended masters also inspired thousands of lectures delivered by the messengers. The content of the dictations are, by most human standards, beyond the mind's ability to construct in real time. They carry very powerful frequencies of light, awakening us to the highest truths we've ever experienced.

We leave it up to you to decide the value for yourself.

Moving toward Your Victory

No matter what path of light you are on, spiritual freedom is attained using tools that have been passed down in wisdom teachings through the millennia: meditation, selfless service, devotional music, prayer, mantra, and the science of the spoken Word. The masters bring an accelerated understanding of these principles, especially suited for the challenges of the modern world, including dynamic decree work and the use of the violet flame.

Next Steps

We are genuinely excited to meet you on the path . . . and hope you are too. We extend a warm welcome from everyone at The Summit Lighthouse, and we invite you to explore the teachings of the ascended masters at our website https://wwwSummitLighthouse.org. Check out our free online lessons and hundreds of articles on a wide range of spiritual subjects. Browse through our online bookstore. And if you would rather talk to someone in person, please feel free to contact us today!